Beginning Again

Beginning Again

TERRY HERSHEY

THOMAS NELSON PUBLISHERS
Nashville • Camden • New York

Published in Nashville, Tennessee, by Thomas Nelson, Inc., and distributed in Canada by Lawson Falle, Ltd., Cambridge, Ontario.

Printed in the United States of America.

Scripture quotations are from THE NEW KING JAMES VERSION. Copyright © 1979, 1980, 1982, Thomas Nelson, Inc., Publishers.

Library of Congress Cataloging-in-publication Data

Hershey, Terry.
  Beginning again.

  1. Divorce—Religious aspects—Christianity.
2. Interpersonal relations. I. Title.
BT707.H47 1986   248.8'4   86-18170
ISBN 0-8407-3075-6 (pbk.)

*Dedicated to two special women
who have revealed God's grace to me
through their lives:*
Gladys Andrews,
my grandmother,
and
Norva Hershey,
my wife

Contents

Acknowledgments

*B*esides being the story of my own journey toward healing, this book is also the story of other people who have made similar journeys. I would like to thank these fellow travelers as well as several people who walked with me along my road to wholeness:

Jim Smoke whose friendship and book *Growing Through Divorce* helped me in my journey;

Dwight Small whose kind words were an important source of motivation;

Robert Baker and the members of the Glendora Congregational Church for standing with me through my divorce and remarriage;

Lyman Coleman whose concern for me offered valuable support along the way;

Roy Barsness whose friendship provided the encouragement I needed to take these steps to wholeness;

my friends at the Positive Christian Singles of Garden Grove whose journeys served as an inspiration for me;

and to my wife, Norva, whose courage and strength of character assure me that God is still a gracious Savior.

Beginning Again—Is There Life After a Relationship Ends?

*E*veryone loves a good fairy tale. Why? Because everyone in a fairy tale lives happily ever after. And there's something about that kind of story that strikes a chord in us; we all desire lives free of complications.

But my life is not a fairy tale. And your life is not a fairy tale. And something that happened way back at the beginning of creation—the sin of Adam—guaranteed that there would be no freedom from complications, interruptions, and failure. We don't need statistics to convince us. We all know what it's like to fail, to fall short of set goals or expectations. Since this is the world we must live in—the "real world"—we must accept the fact that failure is a real part of this world. Failure is not to be ignored, not to be suppressed, not to be denied, not to be spiritualized, and not to be set up as a scapegoat. Instead, failure is to be redeemed.

Failure inevitably produces pain, but that pain is amplified when the failure involves a relationship. I know the pain that comes when a relationship ends. I married "for life." I was a

Christian and a minister. But one day the reality hit—the marriage was over and I was another divorce statistic. *Divorce* had never even been in my vocabulary, but suddenly after five and a half years of marriage, my "partner for life" sat in the room across from me and said, "Terry, we need to talk about a divorce."

The word *divorce* sounded so harsh, so final. Everything inside of me wanted to resist and to say "No!" The decision, though, had already been made, and I knew it.

I had to deal with the impact of her words. The pain that had been eating away at me for months rushed into my heart and mind with full force. Failure in a relationship was no longer "out there." It had happened—was happening—to me, and I hurt more than I had ever thought possible. At this point, trying to discover the theology of divorce didn't help me. I needed the theology of healing and of "beginning again." During the months of my divorce, questions kept coming to mind to haunt me. Is there life after a relationship ends? Can a person who is broken become whole? . . .

The story is told of two men visiting Hong Kong. While walking along the city streets, they couldn't help noticing the number of vendors pushing their carts along the streets in and out of traffic. Attempting to gain the attention of any potential customer, they would shout repeatedly, "Sale! Sale! Good items for sale!" So numerous were these vendors that the two men found it difficult to avoid their aggressive sales pitches. It was for that reason that they noticed a vendor who was different from all the others. He was quiet, staying to himself as he slowly pushed his cart along the sidewalk. So intrigued were these men that they stopped the vendor to ask him about his wares. "What are you selling?" they asked. "Selling?" asked the vendor. "Oh, I'm not selling anything." With that, he reached into his cart and picked up two pieces of a toy that had been broken. "You see, I buy broken things. My joy comes in mending. And that which is mended can be given away where it, too, will bring joy!"

I like that story. Why? Because I know what it's like to be broken. I have seen the pieces of my life scattered. And I have seen the Master Potter slowly, carefully, and lovingly put those pieces back together again. The brokenness in my life came with the failure of a marriage. For you, it may have been the same. For others, it has been the breakup of a different relationship, the death of a loved one, or even the loss of something significant in their lives. This is not just a book about the ending of marriages, but is about what happens to people who have the foundations of their identities pulled out from underneath them. *Beginning Again* is a book for those who desire the fullness of life in the middle of failure, rejection, transition, change, missed opportunities, broken dreams, marital collapse, or death.

This book is for people who know about brokenness, but this book is about wholeness. It declares the good news that the broken can be whole again. Merrill Tenney describes well the men and women that I write to. He remarks that there are few people on the face of the earth who have not suffered heartbreak at one time or another. Some disappointment, some injury, some frustration has left a scar upon their lives that seems ineradicable. Dr. Tenney observes everyone carries the memory of some bitter sorrow or of some shattered hope of the past. But whatever the nature of the trouble, Jesus was sent to aid the brokenhearted, and so are His servants.

I write this book as a testimony to what God has done in my life and to what He wants to do in your life.

Before we go on, it's necessary to take a moment and briefly mention the assumptions upon which this book is based.

RECONCILIATION IS ALWAYS A POSSIBILITY

Although this is not a book about reconciliation, we need to affirm the fact that reconciliation is always our first option. God is a God of reconciliation. If you have not attempted reconciliation, I recommend that you stop and consider that option before you become involved in divorce proceedings. Only after exhausting such possibilities as counseling with a pastor or psychologist and only after much painfully honest soul-searching can any of us consider ending the marriage relationship.

"Beginning again" may be an opportunity to come to terms with yourself, and that new understanding may lead to reconciliation. Tragically, however, many people have lost their opportunity for reconciliation. Perhaps one spouse doesn't care to make the marriage work, perhaps the relationship has been dead for a long time, or perhaps the relationship has degenerated into one that is characterized by physical violence, emotional abuse, or desertion. When reconciliation is no longer a viable option, then we move on.

GOD HATES DIVORCE

Many well-meaning people came to me after my divorce and quoted Malachi 2:16: "The LORD God of Israel says that He hates divorce." It seemed as if these people felt it was their spiritual duty to tell me of God's anger. These reminders made me even more uncomfortable, and the reminders were completely unnecessary. We have misused that verse. It does not say, "God hates divorced people." It says, "God hates divorce." I have one question: is there anyone who doesn't hate divorce?

Of course God hates divorce. He hates it because it tears, rips apart, breaks, and demoralizes. I would worry if the Bible said, "God is apathetic about divorce." But He isn't. He cares enough to hate it.

Because God passionately hates divorce, He offers healing and wholeness to the person who has experienced the pain and hurt of divorce. Unless we have, however, heard God's words against divorce that convict and wound, His words of healing, forgiveness, and redemption will have no meaning. Furthermore, the fact that God hates divorce becomes good news as He seeks to make right what we have made wrong. God still is not

willing to compromise His intention that marriage last a lifetime. God maintains this sanctity of marriage, yet He gra-
ciously and lovingly holds out forgiveness and restoration to
those of us who fall short of His ideals.

DIVORCE IS PAINFUL AND REAL

However obvious that statement may sound, it is a truth
many people choose to ignore. I am writing a book not about a
fantasy or a myth but about a real occurrence that happens in
time and space. We will not be pretending about the pain or the
reality. Besides, such pretending would prevent growth. Only
as we acknowledge the reality of divorce can we put ourselves in
a place where growth will occur. We cannot benefit by denying
our feelings. The healing will come only with our honest and
open confrontation of painful reality. The important result will
be emotionally healthy people who know what causes their
emotions; can attend to, identify, and describe them; and are
free to experience them to an appropriate degree.

GOD IS PRESENT WITH US

The good news for us is that God puts no conditions on His
love for us. He does not require that we earn either His love for
us or His presence with us. He ever seeks us out, pushing us
toward wholeness and wrapping His arms around us each time
we fall. Without His presence, we would be left to our own
strength and power and would be destined to fail. But God has
not left us alone! The Initiator of the healing process is always
with us.

HEALING IS POSSIBLE

We are not merely engaging in wishful thinking or hopeful
daydreams when we strive for wholeness. But we will be

tempted to pretend that the divorce or broken relationship is a dream. In vain, we'll hope for the day when we'll wake up and it will all be over. We'll hold on to this fantasy because healing is a painful process. Healing is also a choice. To be willing to say "I choose to heal" is to be willing to grow through whatever it takes to see change completed.

Now I invite you to walk with me on your journey of beginning again. Your journey may lead to a new understanding of singleness or to a better understanding of your marriage. Most importantly, your journey can lead to a more vital relationship with God and to the wholeness and growth which He offers each one of us.

Chapter One

Crazy Time

THE STORY OF A RELATIONSHIP

They were young. They were "in love."

He was everything a woman would look for in a husband. She was everything a man would look for in a wife.

But, like many, they were insecure and very dependent upon the other. Theirs was a "clinging relationship." Almost without knowing it, they began to cut themselves off from the rest of the world.

Soon the pattern was set. Their self-worth and self-identity were gradually determined by each other, and they became vulnerable to each other's criticisms. The more vulnerable they became, the more afraid they were to retract from dependent behavior. Thus, they confused dependency with "commitment."

Marriage seemed the only alternative. Marriage? "Whatever God wants," they said. They saw no other course. Everything was thought out. Everything made sense. "A marriage made in heaven," everyone said. It seemed so by majority vote.

The premarriage relational pattern continued after the marriage. He was "self-sufficient" and yet attached much of his self-identity and self-worth to their relationship. She played the "mother image," needing to be needed, all the while seeking to find who she really was.

Their freedom to really care was blocked by a wall of self-protection. Even though they hid their fragile egos behind a mutual dependency—interpreted as love—they worked on their self-worth independently and grew further and further apart.

They built the relationship on a selfish motive: guarding an emotional crutch. The marriage obviously failed to develop as a union of two people. It had started out with a disadvantage, and the couple didn't even know.

So they weren't careful. And they killed any possible seed for positive care and love with creeping separateness, self-regard. The emotional support system they had carefully devised soon began to crumble, and the selfishness was exposed.

Disillusionment set in. Expectations were not being met. There was hurt. There was pain. Tears came as they remembered the beginnng, and they mourned the passing of a "good" relationship. Voices echoed in their memories. "You look great together." "You seem so happy."

But their marriage hadn't worked. Where had they gone wrong?

The "Story of a Relationship" is actually my own story. All the emotions of the past sharply reintroduced themselves recently as I reread the journal I began after my divorce. Once again I felt the shock, confusion, discomfort, hurt, anger, and disorientation of the past. Divorce was not something I had planned on. I hadn't put it on my calendar of upcoming events. But suddenly there it was, and with the divorce came many questions. How should I react? What should I do next? What can I do with the pain? Will life ever be the same for me again? All of us who try to recover from broken relationships ask these questions from time to time. And the questions are often followed by tears. We can't understand what has happened and we want some assurance that we will be okay again. The ending of our relationships—marriages, engagements, any kind of personal relationship—is the beginning of what sometimes seems to be a wild roller coaster ride or a mountainous pile of puzzle pieces. The pieces of our lives don't seem to fit together, and any concept of the future is clouded at best. Gail Sheehy had this to say about jigsaw puzzles:

> The comforting thing about assembling the pieces of a jigsaw puzzle is the inexorable logic of it. There is only one choice—the right one. With enough patience, the puzzle can be solved once and for all.
> In life, however, the pieces are constantly changing shape or slipping out of our hands. No sooner do we think we have assembled a comfortable life than we find a piece of ourselves that has no place to fit in . . . sometimes we have to start all over again.[1]

Life is no longer understandable for us puzzlers. It's what Abigail Trafford appropriately calls "crazy time." She explains that, "Breaking up a marriage may be as common as Main Street nowadays, but when you finally do it, the psychological experience seems as uncharted as the back side of the room."[2]

To figure out the pieces of the puzzle, let's walk through the stages of divorce recovery which are part of the healing process. This walk will allow us to see that the stages are natural and normal, that we need not fear the stage we are in, and that we can honestly face where we are now with the hope of moving on.

STAGE #1: Shock Trauma

Shock comes when we face a reality we have not expected. Before we experience shock, though, we sense an unsettling feeling of impending disaster. We consciously or unconsciously realize that an unwanted reality may present itself. Consequently, we attempt to block out all thoughts of what is occurring or about to occur. "This can't be happening to me." "This only happens on TV, or to my neighbors." "No one else in my family has ever experienced this." We do this for self-protection. Our identities are so tied into our marriages that we are neither able nor ready to face the identity crisis that will come with being unmarried and alone.

The result? We do whatever it takes to avoid the trauma. We create padding between ourselves and the reality of divorce. What is "padding"? It is an imaginary wall we build in our minds in order to repress or deny what is going on around us. This is what padding looks like.

Withdrawal

Characterized by moving away from what has been home; by changing jobs, appearance, or clothing; by breaking social ties; by spending most of our time alone (sometimes just sitting in the dark); and by not allowing any of the outside world to break into our reality. At the point of withdrawal, we say, "I want to remove myself from anything and everything that is familiar." For me, it meant wanting to grow a beard and have my hair permed. Why? For a whole new look. I thought the divorce was happening to Terry, so I wanted to withdraw from *that* Terry and become a whole new person.

Busyness

Characterized by becoming involved in everything possible. We let our lives be pulled in many directions. We book our calendars solid, allowing us no free time. Embarrassed to admit that we have nothing to do on weekends, we work late hours, find ourselves involved in superficial relationships, and become easy prey to quick affairs.

In the middle of this busyness, making simple decisions becomes difficult. In the morning, we are unable to decide what shirt to wear. Standing in the grocery store, we forget what brand of milk we usually buy. Why are such decisions suddenly so frustrating? Because our busyness is an effort to avoid the divorce, we've sunk our energies into anything and everything—and due to this preoccupation the simple decisions we face become frustrating tasks.

Dependence

Characterized by a need to constantly retell "my story" to anybody who lends an ear. If the creature has two ears, we tell it our story! If we can keep telling it, we won't have to face the realities we are always talking about.

Bargaining

Characterized by an overpowering need to make things "right." If we can make things "right," we can maintain the illusion that what is happening is still unreal. So we seek to strike a bargain with our spouses and/or God. We make statements such as "I'll do whatever you want," "I'll buy you anything," "I'll be 100 percent committed to you, Lord" or, in the negative sense, "I'll commit suicide if you don't come back"— all of this in an attempt to remove ourselves from the unplanned reality of divorce. Even if reconciliation is possible, bargaining is still merely a protection from hurt because when we bargain we fail to confront honestly the conflict and the pain.

Euphoria

Characterized by excess energy, laughter, and good feelings. As John said in my office only one week after a significant relationship had broken up, "I can't believe how well I'm doing! I'm almost completely adjusted to her not being in my life." There is a sense of release as if a burden has been lifted, and our euphoria convinces us that we will not need to confront reality. The padding does, however, break down, and we move into . . .

STAGE #2: Turmoil

Turmoil is the emotional and psychological reality of having the pieces of life jumbled together so that what used to make sense no longer seems to. It seems the dam has broken, and the unleashed river of emotions is overpowering. We experience a variety of emotions in Stage #2:

- guilt
- depression
- release
- anxiety
- self-hatred
- anger
- loneliness
- confusion
- jealousy
- boredom
- confidence
- relief
- eagerness
- fear
- rage
- bitterness

There is an overwhelming sense that we have lost control! We find ourselves crying at inopportune times; we're prone to behaviors and outbursts that surprise us, and we find ourselves feeling guilty as we shout inside, "Why am I doing these things? I was never like this before!" We apologize to people around us—even strangers—telling them "I'm really not like this!" or "I'm really an okay, together person!" or "I'm usually in control!" All of these exclamations are our attempts to avoid acknowledging that we are in Stage #2: Turmoil.

Why is Stage #2 necessary? Because we need to stop and be honest about what is happening inside us. This turmoil gets our attention and lets us know that something *is* going on which demands that we stop and pay attention. If we don't stop, we'll go on with our lives and pretend that nothing out of the ordinary is happening. This lack of honesty will mean a lack of growth.

How long does Stage #2 last? As long as we want it to. We can choose to make turmoil our lifestyle, or we can choose to experience it and then put it behind us. Here are some suggestions.

Learn to Identify and Deal with Emotions

When I was in Stage #2, my need to explain myself to others was understandable, yet it was common for a well-meaning Christian to let me know that it wasn't "spiritual" for me to be angry and that God would be more pleased with me if I had things "under control." (All of which added to my lack of control!) Rather than these words, I needed to hear the truth that

- emotions are not sins,
- emotions are not unnatural, and
- emotions are not a sign of lack of control.

Instead, emotions are signals created by God to let us know that something is going on in our inner person in the same way that physical pain signals that something is going on in our bodies. If we held our hands over a fire and didn't feel pain, we'd burn our hands. This signal alerts us to what is going on around us. Our emotions perform a similar task as they let us know what is going on inside of us.

The reality is that we have experienced a real loss. In response to that loss, our emotions signal to us that grieving needs to take place and adjustments need to be made. We begin that process by identifying our emotions. We will find this difficult to do, though, if we are stuck with the thought that emotions are sinful or unnatural. If our emotions and feelings are inherently wrong, then our only alternative is to repress them and pretend they don't exist. And like cancer, repressed emotions slowly and steadily kill us from the inside.

Affirmation Exercise:	Emotions are natural, neutral, and normal.

Repeat this exercise to yourself throughout the day. Write it on index cards and place them around your home where you know you will see them. What are you feeling right now? How do your emotions manifest themselves?

The good news is that it is normal to experience all our emotions, which may not be fun or pleasant, but we learn from it. How do we begin? By identifying the emotions we are feeling. This is the first step away from repression. It is saying, "It is okay for me to feel these emotions." Only after we have identified our emotions and given ourselves permission to feel them—and own them—can we choose how we wish to express them. For example, if I own my anger ("it is okay for me to feel anger"), then I'm able to choose positive alternatives for directing that energy.

Begin to Re-examine Thought Patterns

Which come first, thoughts or emotions? Proverbs 23:7 says, "For as he thinks in his heart, so is he." The significance here is that our thoughts control our emotions. Did you know that all of us talk to ourselves? The process has been called self-talk, and that communication goes on in our minds at the rate of one thousand, three hundred words per minute.

Once we identify our emotions, it is important to look at our thoughts because they generate our emotions. Any adjustments and changes in our emotions will take place because of our self-talk. We must therefore examine the self-talk which causes us to continue to generate the emotions we feel. Consider the two possible connections between thoughts and emotions outlined above.

We are following the progression of Column A when we assume that our feelings—those external expressions of our emotions—are caused by an event. When we believe that events directly determine our feelings, then we are at the mercy of the events of our lives. The events themselves seem to control our feelings. In reality, however, Column B is a more accurate pic-

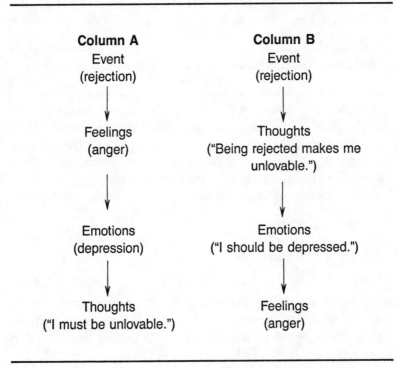

Column A	Column B
Event (rejection)	Event (rejection)
↓	↓
Feelings (anger)	Thoughts ("Being rejected makes me unlovable.")
↓	↓
Emotions (depression)	Emotions ("I should be depressed.")
↓	↓
Thoughts ("I must be unlovable.")	Feelings (anger)

ture of what is going on inside of us: events trigger thoughts and thoughts in turn determine emotions and feelings. Our emotions, therefore, are caused not by events, but by what we *think* about the events. In other words, we feel angry because we've told ourselves (David Stoop terms it *self-talk*) that we are unlovable and that we're unlovable because of our circumstances. Consider for yourself what your thought patterns are saying to you. How are they creating your emotions and feelings?

Look Beyond the Emotions for the Cause

If we want to address our deeper problems, we need to begin by understanding that it is okay to express our emotions! We can get so bogged down in our turmoil that we don't allow the torrent of emotions to teach us anything, and our emotions *can* be our teachers.

Affirmation Exercise: It is okay for me to feel all these emotions.

Initially, as we say this affirmation, we may not believe it or feel that it is true. That's okay. We don't need to feel it at first. Remember that the changes need to take place in our thought patterns. We can still say these affirming statements even if we can't see or feel the healing that is happening.

Having begun to be honest about our emotions, we move on to . . .

STAGE #3: Adjustment

Adjustment is the process of assembling the pieces of our lives once we have decided that we will honestly acknowledge our emotions and the need for change. Adjustment means transition. We're moving from one lifestyle (being married or in close relationship to another person) to another (being single or without that best friend). The following steps can be helpful in the adjustment process.

Practice Positive Self-talk

As Pogo so eloquently put it, "We have met the enemy and it is us!" We need to be our best friends during this time, *not* our enemies. And the best way to begin that process is to monitor what we tell ourselves: we need to monitor our self-talk. Are we telling ourselves that we are unlovable, rejected by God, out of control, and worth very little? Or are we allowing ourselves to begin reinforcing positive truths about ourselves and our growth potential? Are we saying that it's okay to feel all these emotions, that we can choose to grow, and that healing is possible? The kind of self-talk going on in our minds is, after all, our choice.

Learn to Be Creative with Solitude

As we begin to see that busyness is not the answer, we need to allow ourselves to learn the pleasure of solitude. Yes, solitude can become a pleasure! Solitude is our alone time, our personal time, our time with ourselves. We can be creative with solitude, and we can see that it will become a friend.

I recommend that you keep a journal. Record your thoughts and dreams, your emotions and self-talk. Your journal is a way for you to become your own friend as, for instance, you give yourself permission to express your emotions on paper. I've discovered that it's helpful to finish each paragraph in my journal with the sentence, "It's okay for me to feel all these emotions." I also recommend that you read other books by people who know what it means to hurt (there's a recommended list at the back of the book). I benefited by reading from the Psalms in the Bible. To be honest, I wasn't sure God still existed, but in reading the Psalms I was comforted by the reality of a man (David) who was willing to be completely honest with his emotions and who had the courage to believe God loved him regardless of what he had done or failed to do.

Try new ideas with "alone time"—with mealtime, time after work, evenings alone, free weekends. Read a book, go for a walk, take up a new hobby, do volunteer work for a local hospital or church, or plan a candlelight dinner for one. By doing these and countless other things for yourself, you will make solitude a friend. Don't allow loneliness to chase it away. Take the time to list the reasons you can be thankful for solitude, and you'll be surprised to see how that list will grow.

List Your Responsibilities

Often during the recovery process, we find ourselves wasting our energy by assuming responsibility for everything and everyone except ourselves! We assume responsibility for our ex-spouse's behavior, our children's reactions, our friends' responses—and we soon find that these other people control us. To clarify for yourself what you are *not* responsible for and to regain some control of your life, list *your* responsibilities.

This list of responsibilities can now help you notice the many things for which you are responsible. Consider each item on the list of things you think you are responsible for and then ask yourself, "What will happen if I don't do this?" If the answer is "Nothing," then cross that item off the list. You will begin to realize that you have been letting some unnecessary activities consume your energy.

As we define more clearly our real responsibilities, we realize those tasks which are part of being responsible for ourselves. By taking this responsibility for ourselves, we can begin to experience the satisfaction of completing such simple tasks as keeping a journal, cleaning the house, exercising, experimenting with a new recipe, or learning a new hobby. We can also learn to make decisions as we choose to do one thing rather than another.

> **Affirmation Exercise:** I am responsible for myself.

Don't Be Afraid of Failing

Our tendency is to take some of these suggestions and turn them into rules—and then to labor under a sense of guilt because we fail to keep all the rules.

My word to you is, "Relax!" Why? Because I guarantee you will fail somewhere in the recovery process—and probably sooner than you think! But don't despair. The act of failing does not mean that you are destined to be a failure forever and ever—amen! On the contrary, when you fail, you will be forgiven by

God and renewed by His power and love. I'll say it more emphatically. Nothing you could do would alter the fact that God loves you. So don't let the fear of failure keep you from moving forward. The person afraid to fail becomes a statue, paralyzed by fear. When we are confident of God's love and forgiveness, though, we are free to move, free to risk, free to fail.

STAGE #4: Growth/Reconstruction/Redirection

In his book *Growing Through Divorce,* Jim Smoke comments that our growth and recovery happen in much the same way that grass grows. He observes that no one checks the lawn daily to see if the grass is growing, but the grass does grow and suddenly it's time to mow the lawn again. Likewise, we don't look at ourselves daily to see how we are progressing and healing, but suddenly we realize that we have come a long way and that we have taken some important steps toward recovery. When conditions are right, we become living examples of the miracle of recovery.

What are some of the characteristics of growth?

- There is a sense of celebration and a gratefulness for being alive.
- There is both a sense of joy despite pain and the understanding that joy is not the absence of pain, but the presence of God.
- There is a desire to help others in the growth process and to give to others the same comfort we have experienced.
- There is a desire to explore and discover new things, to expand our lives, to get out of the "self-pity closet," and to let life unfold with all that God has in store for us.

CONCLUSION

We have just walked through the stages of the beginning-again process. Having looked at the phases of shock, turmoil, adjustment, and growth, we need to understand that going through the process definitely has its price tag.

Healing will cost *time*. Living in an instant society, we want everything done overnight. Many of us think we will be completely healed just as soon as we've finished this book. In broken relationships and shattered dreams, there is no such thing as an instant recovery. Rebuilding takes time.

Healing will require *perseverance*. There will be times when we'll want to throw in the towel. That's when we need the stick-to-it-iveness it takes to grow through circumstances. We can persevere because God is faithful enough to stay with us even when we feel that we don't deserve it or that we can't go on one more day.

Healing will involve some *risk*. An inner voice tells us, "Don't rock the boat!" Consequently, we tend to remain in a comfortable but unhealthy position rather than risk moving on to an unknown situation—a move that may be uncomfortable for us. No one has said, though, that growth comes easily. Any growth requires taking risks, and in divorce recovery we will be called upon to do just that.

The first question I'm asked after a seminar is, "Terry, how will I know when I'm completely healed?" or "How long does this process of healing take?" Both questions come from an inadequate perception of healing. We assume it's some kind of status or possession. "I've arrived." "I'm recovered." But the stages of beginning again are not like stair steps that we climb one at a time. They are far less clear-cut than that, and it is quite possible we will be in more than one stage at a time. Or we may spend some time going back and forth from one stage to another. Therefore the growth process should be viewed more like a spiral than a staircase, a spiral that takes us on a journey, that points us in the direction we want to go.

In the diagram, opposite, each loop of the spiral contains any or all four of the stages of recovery. This explains why it is easy to move from an acceptance stage back to turmoil. One person

Growth

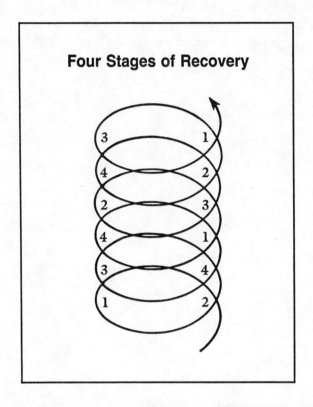

Four Stages of Recovery

said in an exasperated tone, "I used to be in Stage #3. I was able to work on adjusting to the circumstances of being divorced, but now I feel like I'm back in Stage #1 and in a state of shock. What's wrong with me?" Like this person, we assume that we've failed because we seem to have taken a step backwards. It is, however, quite natural and normal to experience each stage at various times as we move along in the spiral growth pattern. I'm suspicious of people who claim that they have no need of healing. "I'm beyond that," one man informed me. As soon as we believe that we've arrived at the top of the staircase, we stop moving. We no longer see life as a journey. We give up any possibility for new growth.

Yes, the healing process is costly but it leads to a new freedom from manipulation by other people, the fear of failure, and self-pity.

────── Chapter Two ──────

Beginning with Honesty

*I*originally wanted to write *Ten Easy Steps to Understanding Obnoxious People*, or *Five Easy Steps to Understanding What Happened to Me*, or *Three Easy Steps to Getting On with My Life—As If Nothing Happened*. But I couldn't write those books because beginning again is not just understanding or learning the easy steps of "moving on." Beginning again is coming face to face with who we are. And that's uncomfortable. We're not sure we want to face our real selves.

But until we do, we play games. We believe myths about healing and beginning again. And if we never face those myths, no amount of new information—no "easy steps"—can make any difference in our lives. Why? Because we're not being honest with ourselves.

That's where we begin, with honesty.

Affirmation Exercise:	The first step of growth is my honesty.

If we were to take a trip by car and needed a map from AAA, they would ask us to tell them where we intend to begin the trip. The same principle applies for beginning again. We can say where we want to go or be—free from the past, in control of our emotions, able to function in relationships—but we're not so sure we want to face the realities of where we *are*.

How do we face those realities? By honestly facing the myths we believe about healing and beginning again. You see, unless we do that, we will be what Scott Peck describes as the "millions of people [who] waste vast amounts of energy desperately and futilely attempting to make the reality of their lives conform to the unreality of the myth."[1]

What are some of the myths we must face?

MYTH #1: Beginning Again Is Like Magic.

There is something inside all of us that hopes for a magic wand. We are looking for the right book— "This may be it!"— or the right tape series, or the right lecture, or the right friend. There's nothing wrong with any of those things, but to assume that any of them will take our pain away is fantasizing.

We live in a microwave society, and we want everything to happen instantly. I remember my first session with my psychologist. His first question didn't make sense: "When is your next appointment?" I was a little put off. "What do you mean, when is my next appointment? There is no next appointment. This is a one-shot deal. You've got one hour to make me okay." And in my mind I thought one session would be all I needed. I was wrong. Ten months later I finished my counseling sessions, glad I had been wrong. Healing is not magic, even though we have our reasons for wishing it were.

"If there's magic, I won't have to face me." A magic wand removes us from the need to look seriously at our pain and inadequacies. We want to be able to get on with life. And we're hoping to find that person whose job it is to take our pain away.

"If there's magic, I won't have to think about these issues ever again." We harbor the secret hope that our past will be gone forever. And when it's gone, we'll be new people.

"If there's magic, I can be normal again." A magic wand will make us legitimate—or okay—again. We just can't believe that we're okay now—in the middle of our confusion and pain and anger and craziness.

But there is no magic. It's a myth. Because magic removes responsibility and says we don't have to face life as it is.

MYTH #2: Telling My War Stories Helps My Understanding and Diffuses the Pain.

This was my favorite myth. I enjoyed war stories. "You won't believe what happened to me!" "That's nothing—wait until you hear this!"

War stories make us feel as if we're getting better, even though we're staying stuck. "But at least I'm talking about it," said one woman at a Beginning Again seminar. "No, you're not," I replied. "You're talking about *him*. There's a difference."

The point is that our ex-spouses' problems are irrelevant to our healing and growth. And past injustices are irrelevant to our healing and growth. War stories only keep us focused on the wrong target. As long as we can blame the "demon" in some-one else, we never have to face the "demon" in ourselves.

In fact, this myth is easily the cause of many divorces. Many people nurture the magical belief that "one can get rid of the unresolved problems of self by getting rid of the person onto whom one has been projecting them."[2]

Does that mean we should never tell our stories? If not, how often should we tell them? My answer is, once. That's right—only once. Let me explain. We should all have the opportunity to tell our stories about what "he" or "she" or "they" did. After that, we're free to tell our stories, but we must tell them with different language. Instead of "he" or "she" or "they," we must begin our sentences with "I feel," or "I am," or "I will." What's the difference? Now our stories are personalized. They are *our* stories. They are no longer "their" stories.

As long as our stories tell what "my ex-spouse did to me," we'll never grow. We'll stay stuck on our war stories, avoiding responsibility, avoiding a look at our reactions and our need for change. We always want to be the "victim." We want people to feel sorry for us. That way we don't have to change.

War stories can be fun, but not for very long. Why? Because they only perpetuate a myth.

MYTH #3: Healing Is for Weak or Very Sick People.

Asking for help is scary. "What will people think of me?" "I can't let anyone know I'm out of control." We assume we don't need "as much help as most people need." Or we repress the fact that we have any needs at all.

By nature, we like to build boxes. We like everything in life nice and neat, understandable and in place. The only problem is that what we're going through right now doesn't fit into any of our boxes. We don't have our act together—and that bothers us. So we work hard at not letting anyone know we're in need. We appear strong. And too often we isolate ourselves so that no one will really see what's going on inside us.

Why are we afraid to let people care for us, give to us, assist us, or love us? Perhaps we don't believe that we deserve help or we don't think we will be able to pay people back adequately. But real love is not based on merit or on our efforts to try to earn that love. And we can begin to understand this truth about love by learning how to receive.

We make the subconscious (and sometimes conscious) assumption that asking for help implies weakness. I believe instead that asking simply suggests that no one is self-sufficient. Asking for help, therefore, is *not* a sign of weakness! In fact, asking for help—being real even in weakness—is the sign of true strength. Now is not the time to be self-sufficient. It's okay to be "weak." It's okay to need healing. That's what it means to be human. Welcome to the human race. The risk of being vulnerable and admitting our weakness *is* scary, but the alternative is unthinkable.

MYTH #4: Healing Is "Out There" Somewhere.

Beginning again happens when . . . When what? When the right person comes along? When the nightmares stop? When the kids settle down? When our friends start to show real concern?

Our minds are filled with "if onlys." "If only I hadn't married her." "If only he hadn't changed." "If only I hadn't said what I said." "If only she would come back." "If only I didn't think about him so much." "If only someone cared." "If only I'd had more time."

If only. All our feelings are real and we can't deny them. But what are we really saying when we say "if only"? We're saying that if our problems were resolved, we could get on with our lives. When our problems are over, life begins. At a Beginning Again workshop, one man verbalized those feelings to the whole group: "I can't wait until I learn these principles. Then I can get past this mess and on with my life."

We can relate to his desire. But unfortunately, the hope that healing is "out there" is a myth. While it's true that the mess we're in will become more tolerable, it's not true that healing means the absence of problems or messes. As one friend said to me, "Terry, life is not the absence of your problems. Life *is* your problems." That's not fun to hear. But it's true.

Does this mean that we'll continue to perpetuate the mess we're in? No. It means that problems are a part of life and cannot be completely avoided. We can wallow in them or deny them, but neither extreme will allow healing. The answer is to face the reality that life is difficult. We must gather the tools of discipline necessary to take our journey, and then make a choice to live "real life"—not a fantasy or a denial. That's what this book is about. Real healing and growth in a real world of pain and difficulty. We don't need to exaggerate our problems to get attention. Nor do we need to pretend they don't exist to appear strong. We can face them—as difficult as that may be.

Life can begin today. Healing can begin today. Growth can begin today. In the middle of our mess and our problems. All of the "if onlys" in the world will not change a thing.

Does that discourage you? I hope not. I hope it's good news that beginning again can happen in the middle of the real world. And beginning begins with honesty. Honesty about the myths we carry and protect. Beginning again means being willing to give up the myths we hide behind.

Are you ready to take the first step?

---Chapter Three---
Who Owns You?

I remember my counselor's blank stare. I had just finished reciting various reasons why I needed to stay married: "If I don't stay married, I'll lose my job" and "How can I continue to be a minister if I can't stay married?" I wanted my counselor to resolve these issues for me.

When he finally spoke, he said, "I understand your need for reconciliation, but not one of your reasons for staying married will help you achieve that goal. You are basing your decision on your circumstances—on the 'if onlys' and 'what ifs.' A healthy decision can only be based on a proper understanding of yourself. Wanting me to rearrange the circumstances of your life is a dead-end street. Your decisions must be based on your desire to get to know Terry Hershey and on your desire to change!"

When I left my counselor's office, I went away with the awareness of an interesting dynamic: we can allow the events in our lives to tell us who we are, or we can find out who we are and see the events as opportunities for growth.

If we choose the second viewpoint, we stand on the biblical truth that events do not determine us. The circumstances of our lives do not have the authority to tell us who we are. Our identity comes from who made us, not from what happens to us.

If that is true, then healing and growth begin in us and with us. You see, I had been so busy blaming my problems on everything around me, I never stopped to look at the only person who could take the steps to begin my healing—me.

While reading a magazine recently, I noticed an advertisement sponsored by the Humane Society. A puppy and kitten were pictured as potential house pets, and the ad read, "It's who owns them that makes them important!" The ad was right—but not just about animals. It touched on the underlying truth about our identity. It's who or what owns us that makes us important. It's who or what owns us that gives us worth or significance. It's who or what owns us that determines whether we are on the road to healing. And we start down that road with the question, "Who owns me?"

Let's pause a minute. Before we begin this journey of "identity-discovering," let me tell you what it doesn't mean.

"Identity-discovering" is not the need to "get my (your) act together" before we can move on in life. It's not navel-gazing for the sake of navel-gazing. And it's certainly not a step backward to the Me-Generation's goal of "finding myself" which served as an excuse for a variety of insensitive, irresponsible, or escapist behaviors. This journey of self-discovery is not to be the next move after a relationship has been dissolved "because we just grew in different directions and became different people." We can't break our commitment to our mates and to God simply because we want to know ourselves better.

Again, as I emphasized at the start of this book, the decision to divorce should come only after we have sincerely and energetically attempted a reconciliation. We should strive for this reconciliation not so much because of what people might think of us or what consequences our divorces might have on our careers. We should strive for reconciliation because marriage is God's creation and we are accountable to Him: we must answer to Him for our actions and as stewards of the people we married.

As I have also stressed, though, once we have exhausted the avenues that might lead to reconciliation and divorce has become a reality, we must then come to terms with who we are. Having just been through an agonizing experience, we need to deal with its effects on us and come to an understanding of who we are and of who we are in God.

"Okay," you say, "but how do I go about developing an understanding of my true identity? How do I get to know myself? How do I come to understand who or what owns me? How do I keep events from determining the kind of person I am?" Together, let's look at steps we can take to discover who really owns us and why.

STEP #1: Identify Your Identity.

Everyone has been born with a little piece of paper inside. On the top of that paper is written "Identity Inventory." On our papers are the people, places, and things we have collected—and still collect—that tell us who we are. These are the lists from which we derive our identities. Unfortunately, most of us have never stopped to examine our lists. Yet everything listed can have consequences on our behavior, thoughts, reactions, and responses.

Everything on our checklists has received permission to be there—by us. And by giving each item the permission to be on our inventories, we may also be giving it permission to have power over us, and to tell us who we are.

Let's look at an example of an identity inventory and its consequences on who we are.

Who or What Owns Me	Consequences on My Life
My past	I feel immobilized. I feel insecure about new relationships.
My former relationships (my "ex")	I worry, because I give him/her all my time, thought, and energy.
My failure	I never feel like I'm good enough. I'm destined to second-best.
My aloneness	I feel unwanted.
My need to make things even (or fair)	I live with the anxiety that all my thoughts go toward getting even.
My friends ("what will they think?")	I guard my words and behavior, afraid of offending anyone.

Now this is only a partial list. Can you think of some items that go on your list? Take some time to list them now. What are the consequences on your life?

The point of this exercise is not to build up excuses for blaming all the people, places, and things that have "fouled up" our lives. The point is to see that we don't need to be blind victims. We're not destined to endure unnecessary turmoil and pain. There are choices we can make about certain things that happen to us. And we begin making choices by being open about the identity inventories we have accumulated.

STEP #2: Desire Change and Growth.

There is a story in the Bible of a man who has been lame for thirty-eight years. He spends his days waiting for his turn to dip into a pool that has healing waters. But before he can manage to get into the water, someone always steps in ahead of him.

When Jesus sees the man, he asks what appears to be a very odd question: "Do you want to get well?" I can easily imagine that man's saying to himself, "What kind of question is that? Of course I want to get well! Do you think I've enjoyed lying around this pool for thirty-eight years? Do you think I get pleasure from this?" Perhaps Jesus asked the question because He knew a fundamental truth about human nature: the presence of sickness does not automatically bring a desire for healing. The presence of a problem such as divorce does not automatically bring a desire for growth or change.

Yes, we may want someone to take the pain away. Yes, we may want someone to alter our circumstances. Yes, we may want someone to tear up our identity inventories. Yes, we may want a magic wand waved over our lives. But we may not want to change. Why? Because change involves responsibility, change involves pain, and change involves the difficult step away from the familiar—however painful or unhealthy the familiar may be.

It's easier to remain in a somewhat uncomfortable negative situation than it is to risk change. Why? Because, as I said, changing means being responsible for ourselves and we would rather have someone else take that responsibility. If that person failed, we could then blame him. As it is, we blame our failure on our circumstances, our ex-spouses, friends, God, families, or anything else we might think of. In fact, the lame man in the story answered Jesus by saying, "I have no man to put me into the pool" (John 5:7).

True change is always based on true personal responsibility. Now, before going on, ask yourself these questions and, more importantly, answer them honestly:

- Do I want to change?
- Do I want to grow?
- Do I want to know myself?

STEP #3: Begin Now—Wherever You Are.

We have already recognized that the first step of growth is honesty. The Bible calls it confession. Confession is not just reciting our sins. It is taking ownership. Confession says, "I own me. My past. My behaviors. My reactions. The good and bad. The flakey and the 'less than desired' part of me." In confession—or honesty—we are free to move, to repent, to change, to turn, to grow. If we're not honest with where we're beginning, what's our alternative? Blame, self-pity, or denial. We're immobilized by what is outside of us.

Affirmation Exercise:	I must own all that I have done and all that I am now.

Part of the process of honesty is the acknowledgment of our present status of singleness. I kept my wedding ring on for quite some time, not really wanting to admit what had happened to me. The journey to wholeness needed to begin with my recognition that I was single and it was okay to begin there.

Affirmation Exercise:	I am divorced (or widowed or separated or brokenhearted—depending on your situation). I am single. I am okay.

Those words may be very uncomfortable or, for some, almost impossible to say. Nonetheless, they are true statements about our present position in life. Just as the paralytic had to acknowledge his paralysis, we must acknowledge our broken relationships and our consequent singleness. Not to acknowledge our condition is to hope and to fantasize that the reality will go away. The reality won't go away, but until we acknowledge that reality, we have no possibility for change or growth.

Facing the reality of singleness can be difficult because today's culture says positive feelings should accompany that reality: we should feel good about singleness. Once again, singleness is an event, or a circumstance, that shouldn't determine our happiness. Rather than trying to manufacture positive emotions, we should work on being honest about who and where we are.

In Chapter 1, we discussed self-talk and the fact that our thoughts create our emotions and not vice versa. This fact contradicts the myth that we must first feel good before we can evaluate our present circumstances. Instead, we can make a positive statement about where we are, knowing that positive feelings will come later.

Remember that where you are is not a bad place to be. Instead it is the place where you can start to grow.

STEP #4: Listen to What God Says about You.

Having understood the importance of acknowledging *where* we are, we can turn our attention toward discovering *whose* we are and what our Creator intends to make of us.

What we hear is the voice of a Creator who cares far more for us than we care for ourselves. Consider the message of Romans 8:31–32: "If God is for us, who can be against us? He who did not spare His own Son, but delivered Him up for us all, how shall He not with Him also freely give us all things?"

Granted, our emotional lives may tell us that those words don't ring true, that God is at best the absent professor. Such responses are normal and okay. For remember, the first step of growth is honesty. That's where we begin.

We must also remember that we're not talking about emotions here. This step is not "*Feel* what God says about you." Our emotions take some time to catch up. We're speaking here about making a choice—often regardless of the way we feel. We can choose to believe the circumstances which con us, or we can choose to believe our roller coaster emotions which bully us, or we can choose to believe what God is saying about us. And He is proclaiming the truth about who we are when He says:

You Are Unique in Creation

King David was overwhelmed by this idea:

What is man that You are mindful of him,
And the son of man that You visit him?
For You have made him a little lower than the angels,
And You have crowned him with glory and honor (Ps. 8:4–5).

In creating you, God said loudly, "You are precious to Me and I gave great care in your making. In creating you in My image, I made you unique and gave you immeasurable worth."

You Can Have Dignity as My Child

"As many as received Him, to them He gave the right to become children of God, even to those who believe in His name" (John 1:12). By accepting His love for us, we are given new identities and dignity as God's sons and daughters. Having before derived our identities from circumstances, things, and people around us, we can now think of ourselves as members of God's family. How can this be? The answer lies in what Jesus did for each one of us.

God originally created people to be His friends and members of His family, but we decided that we could control our own lives and destinies. We decided to live on our own. The Bible calls this pride and selfishness "sin." But God did not give up on His original plan. He sent Jesus to earth to reclaim us as friends and family members. When Jesus became a man, He took on our pride and sin, and they died with Him on the cross.

But the story doesn't end there. Jesus came back to life and through His death and resurrection He offers us new life and a new freedom from the penalty of sin. How can Jesus' life, death, and resurrection become a reality in our lives? We must simply accept Jesus' gift of Himself.

That's difficult to do because we're not used to having someone love us just because he wants to love us. We're used to trying to measure up only to come up short. We're used to opening up to love only to get shot down. We're used to keeping our noses clean for credit only to be told we didn't keep them clean enough. But guess what, says Robert Capon:

> It doesn't matter what the universe thinks. It doesn't matter what other people think. It doesn't matter what you think. It doesn't even matter what God thinks, because God has said he isn't going to think about it anymore. All he thinks about now is Jesus, Jesus, Jesus, and Jesus now is all your life.[1]

How do we respond? By just saying thank you.

If you haven't accepted Jesus' gift, pray this prayer: "Jesus, I've always considered myself to be self-sufficient. Now I know I'm not. I can't make it alone. When You died, You offered me new hope for this life and the right to be Your child and friend. I acknowledge my past selfishness and thank You for choosing to love me for no good reason. I now receive You as the center of my life. Amen."

As My Child, You Have Great Worth

God says it loud and clear: I love you for no good reason! Regardless of what you've done or failed to do, I love you. Listen to the way one of the Bible writers said it: "Knowing that you were not redeemed with corruptible things, like silver or gold, from your aimless conduct received by tradition from your fathers, but with the precious blood of Christ, as of a lamb without blemish and without spot. He indeed was foreordained before the foundation of the world, but was manifest in these last times for you" (1 Pet. 1:18–20).

Once we receive Jesus' gift, we are members of His family. As members of His family, our worth is no longer determined by what goes on around us but by God's constant and unconditional love. Peter's statement is a favorite of mine, and I used to paraphrase it this way: "For you know, Terry, it was not with corruptible things such as your divorce, what your ex-spouse thinks of you, or what others think of you that you were redeemed—or made whole or given your identity—but with the precious blood of Christ. This gives you worth regardless of what you've done or failed to do."

Affirmation Exercise: God loves me for no good reason.

When we choose to believe the truth of God's love for each one of us (no one said it would be easy!), we are on our way to becoming the people God intended us to be!

STEP #5: Identify Those Things Uniquely You.

Now that we have allowed ourselves to acknowledge where we are ("I'm divorced, I'm single, but I'm okay") and have listened to what our Creator says about us, we can begin the process of putting together the pieces of our lives.

We know we need to be honest about how others (including our ex-spouses) have shaped and continue to shape our identities. Now we need to realize that what our ex-spouses think about us isn't important. Why? Because those people do not own us and do not shape our identities. Unfortunately, it's much easier to believe what others say than what our Creator says.

When I think about a person's identity, I like to use the analogy of a credit card. All of us have credit cards which we may let people use in order to be liked by them. Many of us give our cards away without discretion and wait for the bills to come in. Those persons or things we give our credit cards to then own us. To whom have you given your credit card lately?

Why do we foolishly give our credit cards to other people? For their benefit? To prove ourselves? To please people? Take a look at your daily routine and at the things you do, the things you think about, the things you buy, and the things you value. Now ask yourself the following questions: Why am I doing this? Why do I believe that? Why am I buying this? Do these actions and ideas really reflect who I am? How have other people influenced these answers? Whom am I allowing to own me?

Begin to tune into the wonder of you. Yes, the wonder of you! Since your identity is more than what others think of you and what others seem to cause you to do, you are given the exciting privilege of discovering the real you, the unique creation of your Father in heaven. What makes you tick? What are your values? What are your hopes and dreams and fears? What are your goals?

STEP #6: Create New Experiences Based on What You Discover about Yourself.

By not creating new experiences, we force ourselves to draw our identities from current circumstances and negative emotions. Our lives become mere reactions. We allow circumstances to shape us and then we find ourselves feeling caught and manipulated. How do we counteract this?

We begin by making lists of creative things to do in everyday life. Such creativity allows us to realize that we are not bound to present circumstances. Most of us go through life reacting—a defensive posture—to all the circumstances that come our way. The truth, however, is that those circumstances do not have the authority to manipulate us or shape us. Instead, we can choose to be creative within them. Some of my own creative experiences involved reading four books a month, enrolling in classes on new subjects, taking the risk of making one new friend, joining a spa, and making a commitment to a group of people who met weekly for support and pleasure.

At the same time that we add new experiences to our lives, we need to discard what we don't need. Much of what we carry with us is excess baggage. We're tied to many things because of resentment, bitterness, or nostalgia. Does some of your energy go in these directions? Are you using your energy to collect trinkets from the past that will only reinforce self-pity and the sense of failure? Use your energy more productively to reinforce what God says about you and to create positive life experiences.

STEP #7: Be Free to Dream!

A responsible, growing life—one that isn't simply plodding along—requires dreams to give it zest and scope. The energies and motives that fuel both the healing process and responsible living flow from our dreams.

What are dreams? They are mental images of who we can be as God's children. They allow us to see what God desires to do in and through us. They can be pictures of what God wants to make of us.

These dreams don't happen spontaneously. We must choose to make them happen, and we can be as creative as we like. If, for example, you could do anything you wanted with a guarantee that you would not fail, if you had all the money, resources, and talent you needed, and if you believed what God says about your uniqueness in creation and your worth in Jesus, what would you be doing one year from now? Five years from now?

Have you allowed such dreams to be a part of your thought life? If not, perhaps you find such dreams difficult because you don't feel free from the past. If, however, you believe that your worth is given to you by Jesus' gift of His love, and if His gift of love is not based on what you've done or failed to do, then you can be free of the past and whatever mistakes, guilt, or painful memories may hold you to it. Accept this love and forgiveness that God offers! How do you do that? How do you begin to let go of the past? Take the small steps of dreaming new dreams. Share your dreams of the future with a friend. Take a small risk. Remember that failure can't keep you from God's love for you.

STEP #8: Allow Others to Be Part of Your Self-discovery.

We would be remiss if we did not talk about a danger of self-discovery. To paraphrase the words of Henry Fairlie, the danger lies in the fact that the steps from a reasonable self-concern to an utter selfishness are short and swift. As we get to know ourselves, we're tempted to spin little cocoons around ourselves and think we're safe. As we gain self-awareness, we can quite easily become too introspective and very self-centered. Isolation is our number one enemy. It distorts our perspective of life. It exaggerates our problems and fears. It clouds our decision making. It intensifies our vulnerability.

What's the answer? Self-discovery should not take place in isolation from others and apart from relationships of helping and being helped, of giving and receiving. The irony of growth is the simple fact that it begins when we give away a little of ourselves. We may not believe there's anything left to give away! That, however, is simply not true.

Think for a moment how you can begin to give away a little of yourself. You can offer a sympathetic ear, a ride to the grocery store, a simple meal to someone you know, or you can begin a support group. As we open up our lives again, we allow other people to be part of our self-discovery and our healing. Here are some ideas for sharing yourself.

Relationships

We can know about ourselves only as we share ourselves with others. Are you involved in relationships where you can share a little of yourself?

A helpful chapter in the book *Growing Through Divorce* by Jim Smoke is the one entitled "Finding a Family." Its emphasis is upon relationships and how those relationships play a much-needed role in our self-discovery and recovery. Since many of us no longer have nuclear families close by, we need to look elsewhere for supportive relationships that allow us to give a little of ourselves away.

Take an inventory of your relationships. Make a decision to let go of nonproductive relationships (relationships that do not nurture you and may even be negative influences). Focus on making a new friend or reviving an old friendship. Remember that only as we offer our friendship can friendship be given to us.

God's Family

Jim Smoke's *Growing Through Divorce* also directs us to the "forever family"—to God's family. For some of us, this concept is new and unfamiliar. Others of us experience negative feelings when we think of the church. Whatever our response to the phrase "the church," those words remind us of the fact that God does seek us out. He desires for us to be whole and fully alive as members of His family.

Although we often prefer spiritual isolation, God continues to call us into relationships with Himself and with others—into relationships where we can support and be supported, where we can give and receive, and where we can accept others and be accepted ourselves. Deep inside, we all hope for such relationships, but sometimes we don't realize we may be the ones who need to reach out. The question changes from "Who will be my friend?" to "Where can I give a little of myself away and find a supportive place for growth?"

Soulmates

Reaching out to others involves risk: reaching out requires a willingness to let another person be your friend. This friend will walk with you during these difficult times, allowing you to be yourself and encouraging you to grow. I recommend that your soulmate be a person of the same sex. Because of the uncertainty of your emotions, a close relationship with someone of the opposite sex can be complicated by the fact that your need level is high. The fine line between a platonic relationship and a romantic relationship can easily be crossed.

My soulmate's name is Roy. The relationship was not—and still is not—easy. With Roy I had to be honest, I had to confront my pain, and, what was most difficult, I had to receive love. It's because of his friendship and examples of openness and honesty that I am able to write this book today. As my friend, Roy allowed me—sometimes even forced me—to give a little of myself away. He would not let me build a safe cocoon around myself in which I could hide from the world and from other people. I was forced to give a little of myself, and I received a friend in return.

I can't emphasize friendship enough. How do you find such a friend, such a soulmate? You give a little of yourself away; you take the risk that allows you to be a soulmate to someone else.

STEP #9: Accept Singleness as a Gift.

An unfortunate reality that accompanies being single again is the feeling that we are now somehow less worthwhile than we were before and that we can only be restored to wholeness if replacements for our ex-spouses come into our lives. We await the princes or princesses who will appear from nowhere and take us away! As I've said before, though, our lives don't come with such fairy tale endings and healing won't come magically. In fact, healing can't come until we're happy with who we are. Growth cannot come until we're able to be grateful for who we are. And the one fact that we have to come to terms with and even be content with is the fact that we're single.

Did you know, though, that God says singleness can be a gift? When Jesus' disciples heard His teachings on adultery and decided "it is better not to marry," He said, "All cannot accept this saying, but only those to whom it has been given" (Matt.

19:10–11). Later in the New Testament, the apostle Paul referred to his singleness as a "gift from God" (1 Cor. 7:7).

A gift? That's right! We can consider our state of life as a gift of freedom. That means we can choose to grow. We are not destined to be second best. We don't need to harbor resentment. We don't need to feel unfulfilled every day we are single. God sees us as whole! And because He sees us that way, we can be free from all the other voices which attempt to make us bitter and angry and discontented.

CONCLUSION

Why, in a book about broken relationships, is it important to include a chapter on "Getting to Know Myself: Who Owns Me?" You may be thinking, "Let's talk about how we don't have to be lonely," "Let's talk about what he/she did to me," or "Let's talk about how my divorce has really messed up my life." These topics, however, focus on circumstances and, unfortunately, divorce-recovery will not take place merely as circumstances change.

In fact, the circumstances of your life are inconsequential to the recovery process. The circumstances don't matter because recovery takes place only as *you* recover—not as the situation around you changes. As I write this, I think of Jan.

Jan sat in the back of the room with her arms crossed in an almost defiant way. For the first five weeks of my Beginning Again workshop, she sat as if she were daring me to change her. During breaks I would walk by and she would comment, "What you say doesn't work after a thirty-five-year marriage ends!" or "You just don't understand the awful things he did!" At the end of the fifth lecture, I walked up to Jan and put my arms around her. Saying nothing, I just held her. "Not after thirty-five years," she started to say, but then she began to cry tears of sorrow, of confusion, of release. After a few minutes, I whispered, "God loves you." "I want you to help me believe that," she said.

You see, Jan was thinking of the recovery process as something "out there." In her mind, recovery had to do with circumstances, an ex-spouse, the number of years married, or various other details. She had not yet grasped the truth that recovery had to begin with her. What a release she felt when she heard— really heard—the good news that her Creator loves her for no good reason and, with that love, gives her permission to change and to grow.

Like Jan, you have been given permission to change and to grow. Remember, change occurs only as *you* change! Your circumstances are incidental to the recovery process. You must begin with yourself and you cannot do that until you are willing to say, "I want to get to know myself because I want to change and I want to grow. I want to move on, so I'm willing to begin the process of getting to know myself by asking the first question: who owns me?"

---------------Chapter Four---------------

Where Is God?

I remember the weekend vividly. Yes, I had been rejected. Yes, I had failed in a significant relationship. Yes, I was lonely. But my pain that weekend was caused by something greater. From deep within me came the cry of the cross: "My God, why have You left me?"

My prayers bounced off the ceiling. My understanding of God blurred. My belief turned to cynicism. My commitment gave way to indifference. And I felt guilty about all of it. Guilty because a minister shouldn't "lose" his faith. Guilty because a Christian should be "strong." Guilty because I felt I had somehow caused God to leave me. Well-meaning friends said to me:

"Don't worry, Terry. It will pass."

"Just pray about it."

"All things work together for good . . ."

With comments like those, I was tempted to compound my guilt by adding the sin of brutality—I wanted to strangle anyone who came near me with a Bible verse or pious platitude!

I did not need answers; I needed someone to understand. I did not need a Bible verse; I needed the touch of a friend's hand. I did not need more questions; I needed the freedom to doubt.

This feeling that God has left us is common to all, regardless of our religious convictions. It's something all of us have experienced at one time or another: it's the feeling of being utterly alone.

How does the powerful reality of this feeling, when it comes, relate to the things we were saying in the previous chapter? It is important, we claimed, to listen to and understand what the Creator says about us. It's important that we begin the recovery process with ourselves. These things are unquestionably important; they can also be unquestionably difficult. In our struggle to listen to our Creator, to understand who owns us, and to pick up the pieces of our lives, we need to be honest about the times when we are tempted to throw up our hands and say, "I just don't care anymore! I quit! Does all this effort really matter?" And our song can continue with other verses:

"Yes, I believed what the Creator says about me, but now it's Saturday night, I'm alone, and I'm not sure the Creator even exists."

"It's easier for me to give the credit card of my identity to my emotions, to my loneliness, to my depressions, and my circumstances. Where *are* You, God?"

Do these words sound familiar? If we're honest, the answer is yes for most of us. And, once again, such honest recognition is where we must begin. We can't move on by pretending to be something we aren't or by ignoring the very real feelings inside us. We must begin with who we are, however full of uncertainties, questions, and doubts we may be. The psalmist eloquently and passionately raised anguished words to a silent God. I can relate to King David; I've been there, too. Listen to the words of Psalms 10 and 22:

Why do You stand afar off, O LORD?
Why do You hide Yourself in times of trouble? . . .

My God, My God, why have You forsaken Me?
Why are You so far from helping Me,

And from the words of My groaning?
O My God, I cry in the daytime, but You do not hear;
   And in the night season, and am not silent.

When we feel this way, what can we do with our feelings? Where can we turn with our confusion? And why is this experience so paralyzing?

We have all knowingly or unknowingly believed various myths about God. Our world, for instance, teaches us that we need to "feel" God to know that He is real, and that's where much of our confusion begins. The fact is that we don't always feel His presence or His love. This myth and others have added to the confusion that comes when we feel abandoned by God. Perhaps if we face the myths honestly, we can gain some new understanding about the silence of God.

MYTH #1: My Relationship with God Is Not Healthy Unless I Have Positive Feelings about Him.

We've been taught that we need to feel good about God. Of course, that's far easier to say than it is to do. We don't always have good feelings. We can feel like David felt—deserted and discouraged. This myth, however, convinces us that we must somehow manufacture positive feelings. At this point we find ourselves afraid to tell others how we really feel. We walk through life and hide the pain that comes from experiencing God's silence. We don't talk to other people, so how can we talk to Someone we're angry with, to Someone who doesn't seem to care enough to be around when we need Him?

The myth that we must maintain positive feelings about God is a dangerous one because it teaches us to deny reality. It teaches us that God accepts us only on certain conditions, that God is silent because of our inability to manufacture those necessary feelings. It teaches us that God is an eccentric deity who waits to reward people who feel good about Him and who enjoys the opportunity to ignore or punish all the others.

If we continue to accept this myth, we will be unable to be honest about ourselves, and we'll stay stuck in our fear of God and His silence.

MYTH #2: God's Silence Means That He Is Displeased and No Longer Loves Me.

"How could God love me? Look at what I've done!" Shirley's voice grew more intense as she spoke. "My prayers go nowhere. He must be angry and displeased with me. What can I do to make Him love me?"

Shirley was raised on Myth #2. So were most of us. We were taught to believe in conditional love. If someone is angry, she must not love us. If someone is silent, he must no longer care.

This myth teaches us about a love that isn't healthy. It teaches us to avoid anger and conflict because, after all, they only result in the loss of love. Or do they?

As long as we hang on to this myth, we avoid our honest feelings. We will be afraid to say to God, "Where are You?" We will be afraid to say to others, "My faith is growing weaker." We will do less and say less, wanting desperately to avoid the further displeasure of "the gods."

MYTH #3: My Performance Will Please God and Bring an End to His Silence.

If we believe the second myth, belief in this one comes easily. As we contemplate how to get God to love us, we decide that we need to perform, so that's what we do. We feel that God will be pleased with our efforts to earn His love, and our culture seems to reinforce that idea. After all, self-worth is tied to what we do, to how we perform, and to how busy we can be. Surely God, too, must notice all the things we do for Him.

This myth teaches us to deny who we are. It teaches us to pretend to be the people we think God will like. It teaches us that love is earned and that God awards "brownie points" and loves people accordingly. It teaches us that if we "try harder," we might please Him. In the end, this myth brings only discouragement and confusion because now we know even less about who we really are.

In the book of Hosea, we hear God say, "For I desire mercy and not sacrifice, and the knowledge of God more than burnt offerings" (6:6). What's the point of this verse? God's love and acceptance cannot be earned by "right" behavior. It follows, then, that God's silence is not to be understood as a sign of His lack of love for us or of His not accepting us. This point cannot be overemphasized. Listen to author Robert Capon.

> The life of grace is not an effort on our part to achieve a goal we set ourselves. It is a continually renewed attempt to believe that someone else has done all the achieving that is needed, and to live in relationship with that person whether we achieve or not. . . . It is a love affair with an unlosable lover.[1]

Having looked at and discarded some misleading myths, where do we turn now? How can we be certain about this "unlosable lover"? How can we begin to walk through this valley of questioning and doubt? How can we move on, not allowing fear to paralyze us? Let me suggest four guidelines.

Be Honest about Yourself

Thus far we have established a foundational truth: we cannot grow until we are honest about ourselves. We cannot move on until we acknowledge what is going on inside of us. Just like David in the Psalms, we need to be honest about our discouragement, our anger, our fears, and our despair.

We can't be honest, though, if we continually fan the fires caused by the myths we have discussed. Perhaps the most honest statement we can make is, "God, I'm confused, and I seem controlled by myths about You."

This statement is a beginning. It's a step toward wholeness

and such steps are often small ones. This is especially true in our relationship with God. Perhaps you can take this first small step of being honest about yourself.

Affirmation Exercise:	It's okay for me to express my emotions to God. It's okay for me to express (name one emotion) to God.

Fight the Battle in Your Mind, Not with Your Emotions

Believing the myths about God may convince us that the battleground is our emotions. When we believe that, we begin to fight the battle of God's silence and our doubt and confusion emotionally. By manufacturing positive emotions, by performing to please God and others, we hope that the battle is being won. On the contrary, that's a battle we're destined to lose! Why? Because our emotions do not (and cannot) produce changes in us or in our behavior. Change comes from our thoughts, not our emotions.

Since that is true, we need to focus on our thoughts. If they, in turn, point us to the myths, then we will remain stuck and will continue to wonder why our ability to manufacture positive emotions produces no long-lasting change. Our minds, therefore, may need some reprogramming. Do our thoughts point us to a healthy understanding of our possibilities for growth, or do they reinforce our need to pretend, our need to hide, and our need to perform?

Affirmation Exercise:	God's love for me is not based on my performance. God accepts the honest expression of my emotions and does not withhold His love when I express them.

The difficulty we have at this point comes because we have a hard time actually believing those affirmations. In reality, the difficulty is that we cannot *feel* that they are true. But do you see what we have done? We've continued to reinforce the myth that our growth is based on feelings.

Growth comes only as we reinforce truth in our minds. Emotions and behaviors will follow. You may not feel the truth of those affirmations and you may not believe them, but that's okay. By affirming them, we give God the chance to tell us who we are and to free us from being bullied by our emotions. That's called "faith."

Choose to Be Thankful for the Gifts You Have Received

When Bob came into my office, I knew it was going to be a long session. "I'm depressed," he said. "There is nothing good in my life."

"Nothing?" I asked.

"Absolutely nothing!" he confirmed.

"You have nothing to be thankful for?" I prodded him.

"Nothing at all!" He seemed unwilling to budge.

There was a long silence. Then I asked, "Who drove you here?"

"Why, I did, of course!" He seemed surprised.

"Oh," I said. "I just thought if you were so helpless and hopeless that someone must have had to drive you." I went on, "You look nice today. Who dressed you?"

Again he looked surprised. "What kind of a question is that? I dressed myself!"

"I thought you said you had nothing to be thankful for."

"Well, I don't," he said, not so sure this time.

"But that can't be true. You can be thankful that you could drive yourself here. Many people can't. You can be thankful that you dress yourself. Many people can't do that either."

He looked out the window. When he turned back to me, he said, "Maybe you're right."

By the time he left my office, we had a list of twenty things for which Bob could truly be thankful. This is not to say that his depression was unreal. This is not to say that there were things in his life for which he was not thankful. But so often, in the middle of a rainstorm, we forget that it waters the crops.

We hear David affirm this, for example, in Psalm 13. In the midst of his doubt, David nevertheless affirmed his faith in God. He took time to be thankful.

> How long, O LORD? Will You forget me forever?
> How long will You hide Your face from me?
> How long shall I take counsel in my soul,
> Having sorrow in my heart daily?
> How long will my enemy be exalted over me?
>
> Consider and hear me, O LORD my God;
> Enlighten my eyes,
> Lest I sleep the sleep of death;
> Lest my enemy say,
> "I have prevailed against him";
> Lest those who trouble me rejoice when I am moved.
>
> But I have trusted in Your mercy;
> My heart shall rejoice in Your salvation.
> I will sing to the LORD,
> Because He has dealt bountifully with me.

Have you taken a look around you? What can you be thankful for? Children? Health? Friends? The ability to express emotions freely and honestly? Your job? Make a list, and when you are most tempted to despair, pull out the list and read it aloud. Don't deny your real emotions, but don't let yourself believe that confusion and doubt are the final words.

Join with Fellow Journeyers

I enjoy reading the Psalms of David because I feel we have something in common and that's important. Each one of us needs to see that we are not alone in the beginning-again process. Other people feel the same way we do, and we need to join them. The road is not as long when we walk with other people.

Chances are that someone near you needs to hear, "Hey, I know what you're going through. I'm there, too. Do you want to talk?" This could be the beginning of a friendship. More importantly, this could be the beginning of growth.

CONCLUSION

I want to close this chapter with a story from the Talmud which was in *The Chosen* and which illustrates an important idea. The story is about a king whose son runs away. Having gone to a distant land, the son leads a life of squandering and recklessness. Wanting his son to return, the king sends a message and asks him to come home. The son sends the messenger back to his father with the reply, "I cannot return. I am unable to do so." When the father hears this, he immediately responds with the words, "Then, my son, travel as far as you can and I will meet you for the rest of the way."

This story touches the fundamental truth that God does not give up on us. Even when God is silent, when we feel unloved and unlovable, and when we don't know which way to turn, God does not forget us. Such times, however, force us to rely on our intellectual knowledge that God promises to be with us always. We need to cling to this promise despite the fact that our feelings run powerfully counter to this fact: we feel desperately alone and abandoned by God. We need to be reminded—we need to remind ourselves—that Jesus Himself walks with us. He may sometimes walk in silence, but we have His promise that He is always there.

--------- Chapter Five ---------

Failure—Not the Final Word

"You can't tell them you've been divorced," my friend insisted as we were about to go into a meeting where I was to speak.

"Why not?" I wondered aloud.

"Because they will see you as a failure. And who wants to listen to a failure?"

He had a point, I suppose. I could certainly think of more appropriate times, however, to make such a point! Nonetheless, what he had said made me wonder—was I a failure? How was I to cope with the failure of my marriage? Where could I turn? Would life ever be the same now that I had failed at something so important?

I remember my wedding day clearly. My vows were sincere and I expected to keep them until "death do us part." The Bible seemed crystal clear: God's design is marriage for a lifetime and we are not to compromise His purpose for us. My intention was an indissoluble marriage.

There was certainly nothing wrong with that goal. But five years later, the relationship had broken into pieces. In a situation where compromise was not to be allowed, compromise had occurred. Where before divorce had not been an option, divorce was now a painful reality. Where would I go from here?

Having always believed that the Bible is my guide for living, I turned to it for direction and counsel. And I did what most people do: I took a survey of the Bible's teachings. I found three possible ways to look at divorce:

- Without exception, there should be no divorce or remarriage. This seems to be what Jesus says in Mark 10 and Luke 16.
- There should be no divorce or remarriage except in the case of adultery. If one party is innocent of the other's adultery, divorce is allowed. Jesus speaks this way in Matthew 5 and 19.
- There should be no divorce or remarriage unless the unbelieving partner leaves. Paul mentions this in 1 Corinthians 7:12–16.

When my study was concluded, I was confused. How could there be three differing views? The survey seemed to be no help at all. These principles, straight from Scripture, didn't fit neatly together. I couldn't seem to "systematically coordinate" the biblical statements.[1] So I went back to the Bible. This time approaching it without a predefined set of principles, I would let the Bible talk. I hoped to discover a broader picture of biblical morality that would illustrate the individual verses which seemed to contradict each other.

I started in the Old Testament and saw that divorce and remarriage were divine concessions to the weakness, frailty, and sin of God's people. Matthew 19:8–9 both summarized and confirmed this: "Moses, because of the hardness of your hearts, permitted you to divorce your wives."

As I continued to read, the theme that began to emerge seemed to be a framework within which my earlier discoveries began to make some sense. The Bible does not speak of a fairy-tale world. The world it speaks of and to is one that includes failure. The Bible holds out for us, though, the claim and the promise that failure does not have to be the final word. Its message is a message of grace. Grace that comes into a real world and dares to say that failure has no authority. Grace that is part of a living cycle of forgiveness and renewal. Grace that says, "Failure is not to be denied and it is not to be ignored. Failure is to be redeemed. Failure is not the final word." Ironically, this theme brought both relief and frustration as I realized that it was impossible for me to come to a simple theology of divorce and remarriage.

Now what would I do? How could I live without clear answers? Could it be that God wanted to leave the issue ambiguous so that nobody would be able to pin it down and then try to be dogmatic about it? But I was never taught how to live with ambiguity. And yet now the Scriptures pointed me to ambiguity—but it was an ambiguity which ultimately led me to the cross of Jesus Christ.

How did all these ideas help me, a person who had experienced the failure of divorce? First of all, I learned that the answers are not to be found in simplistic principles or self-help books, but in Jesus Himself. I had looked for rules, but I had found that all He asked for was my love.

Second, I realized that I must allow myself to go through the process of forgiveness and renewal. The initial step—the admission that I had no quick answers—was an admission to myself that I had to depend on God. When I looked at myself and my circumstances, my reaction was self-pity: "What an utter failure. I've sinned and, on top of that, the Bible says it's a sin that shouldn't even be allowed. How can I live with myself? I can never be used by God again!" A helpful response? Not at all. It was nothing but selfish pride: although sinners have been saved by Christ's death and resurrection, I was too lost to be redeemed.

By clinging to this prideful self-pity, though, I could avoid taking any more risks and I could avoid caring and loving. I could build a big shell around myself. No one would be able to touch me, and I would be in control. But God does not tolerate such pride. There have been enough martyrs and He certainly didn't need me, with my less-than-honorable motives, trying to add my name to the list.

I had been reminded during my survey of the Bible that the issue in the New Testament is not whether or not I measure up to a standard. The Bible is clear that "there is none righteous, no, not one" (Rom. 3:10). The question, then, is not whether I measure up—because I don't—but instead how I respond to God's merciful desire to renew me. It is basically a question of where my heart is.

This process of renewal was available to me because of God's gracious and generous love for me. An example of this renewal was clearly presented in John 21:15–19, the story of Peter. Good ol' Peter. Foot-in-the-mouth, compulsive Peter. "No, Lord, I'd never deny you," he stated confidently. Little did he know that less than twenty-four hours later he would wish he had never spoken those words. But the story is much more than a picture of Peter. It is a story of forgiveness and renewal. It is the story of the Bible. It is the story of Jesus Christ.

First of all, notice that Jesus allows failure. The story actually begins in John 13:36–38 when Jesus predicted Peter's failure: "The rooster shall not crow till you have denied Me three times" (v. 38). Although Jesus knew that Peter would fail, He didn't stop the course of events. Here is a mystery about the love of God: somehow, He can allow us to fail. He didn't set Peter up for failure. He didn't encourage it or arrange it. Instead, knowing full well that Peter would fail, Jesus prayed for him (Luke 22:32). The significance of Jesus' prayer is His assurance to Peter that He would be with him through whatever happened.

Second, notice Peter's response to his failure. We read about his failure in John 18. The failure is brought into sharp focus when Peter denies knowing Christ for the third time "and immediately a rooster crowed" (John 18:27). As if the failure wasn't painful and disappointing enough, Peter had failed in an area where he had been certain he would not. Did Jesus come immediately to Peter to rebuke him for this failure? Did He recite biblical principles or remind Peter of his promise never to deny Him? The text simply says that Jesus "turned and looked at Peter . . . . Then Peter went out and wept bitterly" (Luke 22:61–62). In the face of Jesus, Peter saw his failure. He saw his inability to measure up to the one standard that is Jesus Christ. He saw his need for repentance.

Genuine repentance begins with the admission that we have done wrong. This repentance will own the failure: I will take responsibility for failing. I will not look to blame circumstances or other people. Having accepted the responsibility for my failure, I then choose to change. Repentance, then, is both an admission of personal responsibility and a newly acknowledged freedom to change.

Third, notice how Jesus reinstated Peter. In a story of simple but profound truths (John 21), the cycle of failure, repentance, and renewal was completed. The setting is the shore of the Sea of Galilee. The characters are the tired and somewhat discouraged disciples who haven't been able to catch any fish. Their luck changes, however, when they follow the suggestions of the Stranger whom John suddenly recognizes—"It is the Lord!" (John 21:7).

Peter, as compulsive as ever, plunges into the water before the fishing boat can arrive on shore. He runs to the Lord, but then stands pensive and uncertain. He knows that he bears the scars of failure. He knows that he has greatly disappointed his Lord, and he is unsure about what will happen next. What does Peter want to hear? What does he expect to hear? Rebuke? Rejection? "I told you so"? Jesus looks into those confused eyes and gently says, "Peter, do you love Me?" Jesus sees Peter's potential and He does not let failure bind Peter. Instead, He calls Peter to obedience and to growth. The call is "Feed My sheep" (John 21:17) and it is a call which does not allow Peter to focus on himself. It does not allow Peter to focus on his failure. It does not allow him to focus on or blame others.

Jesus' call to us is like His call to Peter. Jesus sees our potential and He won't let failure bind us either. Jesus calls us to obey Him and to grow in Him. As we obey His command to feed His sheep, we focus not on ourselves, on our failure, or on other people's responsibilities. We have but one focus: Christ who asks us "Do you love Me?"

If we don't allow this forgiveness and renewal to take place in our lives, we tightly clutch a sorry past and do not allow God to use us. Likewise, when we do not allow forgiveness and renewal to take place in the life of a Christian brother or sister, we place chains of bondage on them. We make them captives of failure, saying, in effect, "We will tell you when you are free to grow."

In his book *Growing Through Divorce,* Jim Smoke makes the important statement that

> God is not in the business of applauding your failures. He wants you to put your trust in Him and be about the business of new beginnings. . . . God is in the business of introducing people to new beginnings. His method of doing this is to bring healing and wholeness into lives through struggle and growth.[2]

In a world which is anything but free from failure, complications, frustrations, or sin, this gospel message is vital. Failure cannot be ignored or denied. We have all experienced failure. We have failed as husbands, wives, friends, employers, employees, parents, and children. The effects of failure cannot be softened or avoided; there are no easy answers. But failure is not the complete picture. Failure is not the final word!

Affirmation Exercise: Failure is not the final word. Grace is always bigger than my failure.

As Christians, our lives are based on another Word: our lives are based on Jesus Christ. Like Peter, we need to stand face-to-face with Christ and accept the reinstatement He offers us. Have you, like Peter, allowed the process of grace and renewal to take place in your life? Or have you given failure more authority than it deserves? Have you confined yourself or anyone around you to a prison cell of failure? Failure is not the final word! In Jesus Christ, the final word is grace. And because of that word, failure has no authority.

------------------- Chapter Six -------------------

Freedom to Forgive
and Be Forgiven

*F*orgiveness is the key to unlocking the full healing process in divorce recovery, yet forgiveness is difficult to understand, easy to ignore, and uncomfortable to talk about.

The word *forgiveness* makes the mind engage in some interesting gymnastics. We hear statements such as . . .

"Sure, I'll forgive. But let's wait until so-and-so shows a little repentance for all he did to me!"

"Forgive? Maybe. Forget? Never!"

"How can God forgive me for what I've done?"

"How can I forgive my ex-spouse? Did I tell you everything he/she did to me—and to the kids?"

"Me? Be forgiven? But how could God forgive me? And how can life ever be the same again?"

"I would like to forgive her, but I don't know how."

"To err is human, to forgive is out of the question!"

As we look together at our need for forgiveness and our need to forgive, it would be helpful to show the cycle of thoughts and emotions which comes with the hurt of a divorce (in the diagram on page 72).

How do we break this cycle? How can we get off this vicious merry-go-round? Is there any hope?

WALKING THROUGH THE STEPS OF FORGIVENESS

Be Honest About Your Struggle to Forgive and Accept Forgiveness

Let's review. We're tempted either to deny our problems or to magnify them beyond reasonable proportion. Why? Because we don't want to face reality. And we don't want to face reality because dealing with reality will require dealing with responsibility and change.

We need, however, to face honestly and directly the reality of hurt in our lives. It has occurred and avoiding that fact will not help us heal. Pretending that the pain will take care of itself will not help us heal. Only honest acknowledgment—"I was a part of the relationship that failed, and the resulting hurt is very real"—allows us the possibility of moving on.

Affirmation Exercise:	My hurt is real, and I am struggling with the issue of forgiveness.

Be Honest About Your Role or Part in the Hurt

Our tendency is to say, "But what about . . . ?" We try to make sure that someone else is responsible for us and our misfortunes. You see, if we can blame something or someone else,

Hurt

Whether it stems from a divorce, a broken engagement, or the rejection by a friend, hurt is real.

Self-Talk

We reinforce the guilt by continuing to focus on negative self-talk.

Guilt and Self-Justification

After we have attempted forgiveness, we feel like it "didn't work." We feel that we don't deserve forgiveness and that the other person doesn't deserve forgiveness. We feel guiltier now because we can't even forgive without failing.

Emotional Logjam

Turmoil is natural and normal. It signals that we have experienced loss and that grieving must take place.

Self-Talk/Remembering

We reinforce the hurt by continuing to focus on negative self-talk.

Guilt

We feel guilty because we "should" be strong and in control and because we "shouldn't" be angry with God.

Attempted Forgiveness

We attempt to forgive the one who hurts us. We say, "I forgive that person" and think that we have resolved the issue by merely reciting some words.

we can avoid having to focus on ourselves—on our weaknesses, our failures, and the need to change.

Unfortunately, change comes only as we are honest with ourselves about ourselves. And the truth is simple: we are part of the problem. No matter how little we feel we contributed to the problem, we're still a part of the problem. Circumstances and other people are the givens of our lives, and we often have little, if any, control over them. We may therefore think of ourselves as victims. We do, however, have some control: we control our responses to circumstances and our responses to people.

> **Affirmation Exercise:** I accept responsibility for myself and my failures. I am part of the problem.

Acknowledging our contribution to the end of the relationship is never easy or painless. I am reminded of Bob. As he sat in my office, he made the purpose of his visit clear. "Pastor, I need you to help me get over my divorce."

"I'll do what I can," I responded. "Tell me, Bob, what do you feel?"

"What do I feel?" He seemed surprised. "What should I feel after what she pulled?"

"You sound angry."

"Angry? No, I'm not angry. I just can't understand her. Why did she do this? Our marriage was doing fine until she started getting these crazy ideas about her independence."

"That would hurt me," I offered.

"What's important," he continued, "is understanding her crazy behavior."

This conversation went on for an hour. I knew we would make no progress. Why? Because Bob was unwilling to focus on himself, unwilling to focus on the reality of his hurt, and unwilling to focus on the reality of his role in that hurt. He was stuck, and he was destined to remain in a fantasy that began with the words, "But she . . ."

Being honest about our part in the hurt is not easy or enjoyable. One woman came up to me after a workshop and said, "I was doing okay until I came to your workshop." I understand her frustration. We want to have everything nice and neat. We want to know who did what to whom. We want to assign blame.

This is a temptation for Christians, because we want to have "biblical divorces." That means that one person in a failing marriage is to blame and the other is a victim. I was encouraged to think along those lines by friends and a former employer. But I said to them, "Wait a minute. Are you saying that I should try to prove that she wore the black hat and I—the helpless victim— wore the white hat?"

Such a need to balance blame is wrong. The fact is simple: each of us has contributed to the failure of our marriages. Dividing up percentage points is irrelevant. Granted, someone may be "more to blame." But until we all take 100 percent responsibility for our participation, we will not grow or move on. We will stay stuck to our need to blame.

Some of us go to the extreme of taking all the blame. Is that helpful? No. In fact, it's a cancer that causes resentment, because we don't get enough attention for "taking the blame and letting her/him get away scot-free." Self-blame always produces self-pity. But responsibility always leads to the opportunity for change. Responsibility allows movement and growth. "Up until now . . ." is the dialogue of people taking responsibility for their behavior. "Woe is me . . ." is the dialogue of people wallowing in their past mistakes.

Perhaps we're afraid to accept responsibility because we don't think we have any hope for forgiveness. So we "self-blame," because after all, we "had it coming."

In Psalm 51, we find an example of someone who was willing to admit his role in the hurt. David was painfully aware of his sinfulness and took responsibility for it through confession, knowing that God would accept him.

Have mercy upon me, O God,
According to Your lovingkindness;
According to the multitude of Your tender mercies,
Blot out my transgressions.
Wash me thoroughly from my iniquity.
And cleanse me from my sin.

For I acknowledge my transgressions,
And my sin is ever before me.
Against You, You only, have I sinned,
And done this evil in Your sight.

(Psalm 51:1–4)

Forgiveness—both offering it to others and accepting it from God—is possible only when we acknowledge our role in the situation which resulted in hurt and offense. We need to begin where we are now: we need to begin by accepting the fact that we contributed, if only slightly, to the breakup of an important relationship. Our focus must be responsibility—not blame, not outraged innocence, not pointing the finger, not self-defense—but personal responsibility.

Allow God to Forgive You

As we examine our role in the hurt, we realize that we are guilty parties and that it really doesn't matter how guilty our ex-spouses may be. Our guilt tells us that we have the need for change. It helps us see our failure, our weakness, and our sinful nature. We realize that we didn't do what we wanted and that we did do what we didn't want. Listen to a frustrated Paul wrestle with this very issue: "For what I am doing, I do not understand. For what I will to do, that I do not practice; but what I hate, that I do. . . . But now, it is no longer I who do it, but sin that dwells in me" (Rom. 7:15–17).

Our guilt also tells us that we need Someone bigger than we are who will free us from this guilt, from this burden, from this ball and chain to the past. How can we be set free? We simply need to accept God's forgiveness. Even more basic, though, is our need to understand this gift.

First, we must understand that within each of us is the image of our Creator. Through the ups and downs of our lives, our Creator is seeking to perfect that image in us. The Bible calls it "Christlikeness"—or maturity, bearing fruit, being fully alive, and being whole.

However, we decided long ago (and each of us decides daily) that our way is better than God's way. The result is sin. Rooted in selfishness and pride, this sinfulness is the desire to be in control. It is the desire to have our world neatly defined in such a way that we feel we are self-sufficient and able to manage anything that comes our way. What is the result? Broken relationships with God and with other people.

As a result of this estrangement, we need to be reinstated to wholeness. The Bible calls it being redeemed, being reconciled to God, and being made right with (or at peace with) God. We are thereby given worth by God. We don't need to perform for Him; we don't need to earn His love.

Instead of resulting from any effort on our part, reinstatement comes when we recognize that we don't have the ability to make ourselves whole again. We need God to perform that miracle for us, and He does so in Jesus Christ. The Bible tells us that Jesus took the punishment for our sins. Through the death and resurrection of Christ, we are reinstated. The good news is that this reinstatement is a gift—it is free of charge! We have only to ask for it.

We ask for this gift by our repentance, by giving control of our lives back to God. Repentance is the act which says

- I own responsibility for my part in the pain.
- I own who I am.
- I own what I have done.

And yet in repentance, we give control of all these things back to God. If we don't repent, we are by necessity controlled by the past, by our need for revenge, by our hurt, by our self-pity, by our pride, by our sin. Receiving forgiveness is letting God tell us that our identities and self-worth are bigger than our need to perform or our need to get even, or feel sorry, or define ourselves by our failure.

The gift of God's forgiveness through Jesus Christ frees us from these and other forces. Forgiveness means that we are free from our sins, free from the past, free from our need for revenge, and free from pride and self-pity. We are forgiven!

In his article "Divorce and Remarriage: A Fresh Biblical Perspective," Dwight Small commented:

> All divorce is failure to meet God's standard and hence it is sin; all parties alike need God's grace. But to all divorced Christians, guilty as well as innocent, renewing grace is available. The sole condition is true penitence, confession, and the sincere desire to go on to fulfill God's purpose.[1]

Until you allow God to forgive you and grant you freedom to move on, you will be allowing such feelings as guilt, hurt, resentment, or self-hatred to control you, to tell you who you are, and to give you your identity.

Receiving forgiveness is difficult for us because we want to believe we are still "in control." I attempted to stay in control of my life by asking God to "excuse me" rather than "forgive me." I wanted him to "let me off the hook" because I wasn't the bad guy, or because I tried harder. I was always attempting to marshal a case in my defense. I realized it was getting me nowhere. In effect, God was saying, "You don't need to impress Me with either your innocence or your martyrdom, because you don't need brownie points with Me. I've already seen where you've failed. But I love you regardless. I don't want to excuse you. I want to forgive you and allow you to begin again."

Do you wish to receive this gift of forgiveness? If your answer is yes, then I want you to know that the gift of forgiveness is available. It can be yours today. I invite you to pray this prayer with me: "God, I know divorce is wrong. I know that it was not Your ideal for me, and I take responsibility for my part. I confess my weaknesses and my conscious and unconscious contributions to the failure of my relationship. I know that I chose to act as if I was in complete control. God, I ask for Your forgiveness for my failure. I ask for the forgiveness which is available through Jesus Christ. As I receive that gift of forgiveness, I accept the freedom to move on and to give up my need to blame. Help me to experience Your love and lead me to new growth and new beginnings in my life. Thank You, Lord! Amen!"

Having prayed this prayer, be confident of God's forgiveness. In the days of the Old Testament prophet Jeremiah, God promised, "I will forgive their iniquity, and their sin I will remember no more" (Jer. 31:34). This promise is reaffirmed in the first epistle of John: "If we confess our sins, He [God] is faithful and just to forgive us our sins and to cleanse us from all unrighteousness" (1 John 1:9). You *are* forgiven! Granted, you may not feel it. But remember, forgiveness doesn't begin with feelings. It begins with a choice.

Forgive Yourself

If God has forgiven us, then we certainly ought to be able to forgive ourselves. Unfortunately, we often choose to lock ourselves in a self-imposed guilt chamber, tormenting ourselves with the thought that "If only I had . . . , things might have turned out differently." We're afraid to forgive ourselves. Why? Because then we would be free. And, as I have said before, that calls for responsibility and responsibility is uncomfortable.

Sarah had gone through a very traumatic experience of physical abuse. Understandably, she was finding it difficult to face what had happened. Added to that difficulty was a strong sense of personal guilt. "If only . . . ," she would say. Sarah couldn't forgive herself. She took the entire blame and kept it stored inside her heart.

"See, I told you I was worthless," she would often say, and

our attempts to convince her of God's love and forgiveness seemed entirely useless.

"If it's so painful," we wondered aloud, "why are you hanging on and beating yourself over the head with it?"

After a long struggle, the truth came out: "I don't want to let go. It's the best story I've ever had."

There is something of Sarah in each of us. We are afraid to give up our hurts and failures: we want to use them to reinforce a low self-image. And we hang on to this poor self-image because we are afraid to receive love. This way of hiding behind our failures can also be called self-pity, and the line of thinking runs something like this: "Because I don't feel good about myself—after all, I'm a failure—I can't understand how you can love me. I thereby offer you a reason not to love me as I hide behind the failure and the hurt."

Rather than receive friendship and love from people around us, we prefer to punish ourselves. We act out the self-fulfilling prophecies that say we are unlovable and worthless failures. We hurt ourselves more and then hide behind that ever-growing wall of hurt—all because we are afraid to let God love us and because we are afraid to love ourselves.

But it doesn't have to be this way. We can change. We can be forgiven. We can forgive ourselves. We can move on.

Affirmation Exercise:	My hurt is real. I have been given the freedom to fail. I accept responsibility for my failures. I can and will begin again.

Give Up Your Fantasies

When we decide to quit playing the "blame game" with ourselves, we realize that the game can no longer be played with our ex-spouses or our circumstances. Being forgiven and accepting that forgiveness free us from our need to blame, free us from the guilt of our past, the self-pity of the present, and the immobilizing fear of failure in the future. If we aren't comfortable with this freedom, though, we may hang on to certain fantasies in order to avoid responsibility.

FANTASY #1: Blaming ("It's All Your Fault!") Will Help Reduce the Pain.

We believe that pain is transferable so we blame other people for our situation. Unfortunately, blaming only serves to harden the pain by keeping us chained to the need to find a scapegoat.

FANTASY #2: Ritualistically Repeating a Magic Apology ("I'm So Sorry.") Will Release Us from Binding Misunderstandings.

This fantasy keeps us from being honest about the hurt and helps us pretend that life can go on without our having to take a realistic look at the consequences of the hurt. As I've said before, we can't move on until we can be honest about where we are.

FANTASY #3: Atoning for the Broken Relationship ("I'll Make It Up to You!") Will Repair It.

One version of this fantasy is the "I'll make myself a doormat" offer. We may, for some reason, feel that there is a valid reason for the hurt that has happened to us. If we punish ourselves enough (by letting ourselves get trampled by other people, for example), we then can feel that the bigger hurt was what we deserved. We hope that putting ourselves in this subservient position will be an important step toward rebuilding the relationship.

FANTASY #4: Avoidance ("If I Don't Talk about It, It Won't Hurt So Much.") or Denial ("Problem? What Problem?") Will Make Reconciliation Easier.

The reality, of course, is that such avoidance only buries the situation where it will ferment and later rear its unwanted head in places and at times that are both inappropriate and unexpected. Repression does not solve anything.

FANTASY #5: Displacing the Pressure Will Ease the Pain.

We may gossip ("Have you heard the latest?") to relieve some pressure. We might take out our frustration and vent our anger in more violent ways, and innocent parties will suddenly be the victims of our outbursts. We might also share our thoughts and feelings because of the growing sense that the more we talk about our situation, the less we have to feel the pain of it all. Our divorces become impersonal stories rather than very personal wounds which require our honest attention.

FANTASY #6: Forgetting ("You Know, I've Forgotten about the Whole Thing!") Will Somehow Remove the Pain.

We enjoy this fantasy, and we nurse the hope that we can remove ourselves from a part of reality. We let ourselves believe that forgetting is "better" for us. Unfortunately, our emotions don't understand the fine-tuned reasoning of our intellects, and we suffer the effects which repression can bring. The fact that the head can understand doesn't mean that the heart has healed. The emotions of the heart need to be experienced—they need to be felt—so that they don't eat away at us.

I'll be honest. It really makes me angry when a well-meaning Christian walks up to me and tells me to "forgive and forget."

So I spend all my energy trying to forget—because after all, that's "Christian," isn't it? Then why do I need to keep reminding my friends of all the things "I have forgotten"? And if I have truly forgotten, why do I need to forgive?

We are, therefore, never called to forget. To desire to forget is based on a desire to cut out a portion of our lives and say, "That did not exist." This is the "amputation method" of divorce recovery. What has happened is and always will be part of us, no matter how desperately we might want to forget the events. We can't cut out that part of us, and the good news is that we don't need to. God wants us whole. Until we give up our fantasies, however, they will only be roadblocks on our road to wholeness.

Forgive Other People Including Your Ex-Spouse

To forgive is to say, "You are free from my need to hurt you back, my need to seek revenge, and my need to hold you solely responsible for the broken relationship. I am now free to move on. I am not chained to the past, to self-pity, or to you."

The need for revenge does tie us to the past as this 1982 story from the *Los Angeles Times* illustrates. The headline read "Idaho Youth Slain by Other Prisoners—Mother, Trying to Avenge Son's Death, Sues Jailers." The journalist quotes her as saying, "I promised Chris (her son) on his deathbed that they would pay, every damn one of them, and they will. . . . It's all I think about, all my life is filled with. There is nothing else for me." The article went on: "A heavyset woman of 40, she is committed to a single goal: revenge. She savored the word."[2]

Without realizing it, we too can easily fall into the trap of wanting revenge and needing to hurt back. Although we might think that we're in control, it soon becomes apparent that we are "the controlled" and our need to get even is the unrelenting taskmaster. "Holding a grudge is a subtle form of suicide," said the Reverend John Palmer, director of Christian Education at

New York City's historic Trinity Church. "It's clutching that little piece of garbage so tightly that that becomes almost your *raison d'être,* and you're defining yourself in a negative way."[3] Only forgiveness can free us from this need to get even, this need to make things "fair," this need to seek revenge.

Forgiveness will also allow us to change and to be changed. There is a myth in divorce recovery which says that we need to understand what happened. We want all the pieces of the puzzle to fall into place. We ask ourselves unanswerable questions and torture ourselves with cries of bewilderment: "How could someone who loved me leave me?"; "I thought I knew her!"; "That behavior—it's just not the person I married!"; and "How could something so good turn into something so bad?"

There is an irony in this process: understanding the situation would neither remove the pain nor allow us the freedom to change. It would only result in a continuous mental rehearsal of sentences which begin with "If only I had . . ." Therefore, don't seek to understand the situation. (Besides, to forgive, you don't need to understand!)

If you do not seek to understand the situation, what are you to do? You seek to be understanding of the person. What is the purpose, though, of being understanding of him or her? This attempt to be understanding will help you see the difference between what the person *did* and who the person *is.*

What, then, are the steps you need to take so that you can be forgiving and understanding?

- Believe that you yourself stand forgiven before God.
- Give up the "blame game": stop blaming yourself and your ex-spouse.
- See his/her worth through God's eyes. You may not understand him or her very well. You may not see (or may not want to see) that person's worth, and you may not want to forgive. God, however, sees the worth of every person and He forgives us all. As He asks you to see worth in your ex-

spouse and to forgive that person, He also asks you to rely on His ability to help you see that worth and want to forgive. Here you give control back to God.

* Forgiveness is a choice, an act of the will. Choose, therefore, to forgive. Make the decision both to free your exspouse from your blame and to free yourself from your need to get even. Rely on God for strength to stand fast in this decision. Rehearse your choice mentally and verbally. Say aloud, "I forgive you, _____. I release you from my need to get even, from my need to hold you solely responsible for the situation."

You may never get an opportunity to say this to the other person. Or if you express your forgiveness, that person may refuse to receive it. But remember that the person's response does not invalidate the forgiveness process. The forgiveness frees you. And, just as that person's response doesn't invalidate your choice of forgiveness, neither do your own feelings. Your feelings may contradict your choice, but don't allow these feelings to discourage you. You may not feel like you've forgiven a person, but that feeling does not make your choice invalid. You can choose to forgive a person and then you can choose to let your self-talk confirm either the choice to forgive or the feelings which contradict that choice.

CONCLUSION

In considering all that has been said about forgiveness, we must remember that false forgiveness

* denies the real anger that exists,
* acts as if the hurt never happened,
* smiles as though the end of the relationship never hurt,
* pretends that all is forgiven.

The nature of true forgiveness is quite different. True forgiveness, as I've said, is a choice, not a feeling. We can choose to forgive even when we do not "feel" like it.

True forgiveness also requires reinforcement. We must make the choice daily. Let's be clear on one thing: forgiveness is never a one-time, once-and-for-all activity. It is not easy. Forgiveness is, in that sense, "aerobic": it is an activity that requires consistency, time, practice, and effort.

True forgiveness will be a slow process, taking place one step at a time. True forgiveness cannot be rushed or hurried, so we must not expect instantaneous growth. We may feel frustrated because we have not yet successfully reached the point of being able to forgive our ex-spouses. That's okay. Remember, it's important that we began where we are, and many of us have not taken the first step. We have not yet been honest about our struggle to forgive and be forgiven. With time and the genuine desire to forgive, though, we will one day be able to forgive and we will experience healing and growth in ways we never imagined.

Chapter Seven

Letting Go of the Past

He couldn't have been more serious. He sat across the restaurant table and continued to exclaim: "I can't believe how good I feel! It's amazing! I've forgotten everything about her. It's like the whole episode has been erased from my mind and my memory. It's a fresh start for me!"

The fact was, though, that it had been only three weeks since Jim had broken up with his fiancée after dating her for five years. In reality, Jim hadn't forgotten. He was repressing his pain instead of dealing with it.

I decided to ask him a question. "Would it shock you if I told you it isn't possible or healthy to forget everything in your past?"

"Why remember?" he asked. "What good can it do? If your past is your enemy, why not be rid of it?"

"Because," I answered, "your past is not your enemy. It's what you think about your past that can be an enemy. At this point, Jim, you are your own enemy."

As Jim and all of us have realized and as Mel Krantzler so aptly phrases it, facing the past is not easy: "Among all the dilemmas divorce poses, the power of the past is the hardest to understand and, once understood, the most difficult to overcome."[1] I see the truth of this statement confirmed weekly as people verbalize their feelings with such remarks as:

"I just can't seem to get him/her out of my mind."

"I'm trying to remember only the good things that happened."

"I thought I had forgotten everything—but little reminders keep popping up."

"Will I ever get past this battle in my mind?"

In his book *Creative Divorce,* Mel Krantzler outlines three basic facts:

- No divorced man or woman is immediately free from the past. Such freedom only seems possible when there is a complete and unhealthy repression of the past, but repression cannot lead to freedom.
- We need our past. It gives us a sense of identity and history. It is a significant part of who we are and a sign of what we can become.
- We must not give a disproportionate power to the past. Simply put, we can stay connected to our past without letting it have power over our present lives.

In reality, however, when most of us face the issue of our past, we come up with two alternatives which deny the truths just set forth:

- We continue in bondage to relationships that no longer exist. This is characterized by dependence, bitterness, hostility, and many other unhealthy responses.
- We attempt the "amputation method" of recovery and strive for a complete break with anything and everything of the past.

The first alternative is intolerable; the second is usually unattainable, as well as undesirable and unhealthy.

SO WHAT DO WE DO?

The illustration has been suggested that after a divorce, we want, with a single swing of an axe, to cut the thick cable which connects us to our past. We feel, though, that we have been given a pair of wire cutters and can only snip certain strands of the cable.

So how can we begin cutting? Where do we start? How long will the process take? Let's look at the various strands which connect us to our past. Let's look, too, at the process by which we can successfully cut them. Be advised before we start that, ironically, we may find ourselves devoting more thought, more energy, and more emotion to our old relationship than we did during the years of our marriage!

DECEPTIONS THAT NEED TO BE RECOGNIZED

Before we can cut the strands that connect us to our past, we must come face-to-face with some deceptions that can prevent a healthy recovery.

DECEPTION #1: "I Must Forget about the Relationship."

This deception claims that denial is both healthy and necessary. By forgetting the past and wiping it all out of our minds ("Divorce? What divorce?"), we will be free from our past.

Unfortunately, once repressed, the past is more harmful to us and to those around us. Why? Because the emotions are still there. We may have pushed them beneath the surface in the same way that we push a beach ball under water. When the emotions come to the surface (and they will), the outburst may be quite violent and destructive. Besides the delayed and more intense reactions, denial can also result in ulcers and anxiety, a constant need to remind others that we've "forgotten," and a sense of guilt whenever we realize that we really haven't forgotten.

DECEPTION #2: "I Can Just Leave the Relationship Behind and Move On."

This deception tells us that we can take our past, roll it into a neat package, set it on the shelf, and go on with life. The attraction of this deception is understandable and, because it is partially true, quite powerful.

We are able to go on with life, but this ability to move on is dependent upon our capacity to deal honestly with our past. I call this the ability to pay our emotional bills. Forgiveness is the currency we use to pay these bills. By our earlier definition, forgiveness means dealing honestly with the hurt and the past. Trying either to forget the past or leave it behind keeps us from dealing with the hurt in an honest and healthy way. Forgetting is, however, a means of avoiding the subject of responsibility and therefore is a more appealing and considerably less painful option.

DECEPTION #3: "If the Past Ever Comes Up, I Can Simply Ignore It."

This is based on the assumption that we are capable of selectively weeding out certain memories and emotions of the past. Unfortunately, this is not as easy in practice as it may look on paper. The energy it takes to repress thoughts selectively is energy which destroys us.

A	**C**
(Activating Events)	(Emotional and Behavioral Consequences)
My spouse left me. ⟶	I must be an unlovable person.
My children are angry with me. ⟶	I must be a bad parent.
My friends avoid me. ⟶	I must have done something wrong; I must not be able to be a good friend.
I'm divorced—and I never thought that would happen to me. ⟶	I am a failure. I must be incapable of a lasting relationship.

GETTING THE PAST IN PERSPECTIVE

How, then, can we avoid giving a disproportionate power to our past? Denial or repression will not work. Instead, I believe, the solution is self-talk, a concept we looked at in Chapter 1. How our wounds heal is up to us, and our self-talk can dramatically affect the process. The basic principles for effective healing which I would like to recommend are taken from Dr. Dave Stoop's book *Self-Talk*. Let's begin by looking at the ABC's of our emotions.

As we look at the past in an attempt both to understand it and to seek freedom from it, our attention is most easily drawn to circumstances and events. In the diagram above we refer to these "Activating Events" with the letter *A*. (See the left-hand column.) There is certainly no denying the reality of activating events in our lives. They would not cause us alarm, however, were it not for the consequences they seem to bring to our lives. We will let *C* represent these "Emotional and Behavioral Consequences." (See the right-hand column.)

Let's take a moment to consider what this chart suggests about the way we think. The design itself implies that $A = C$, that activating events in our lives lead directly to our emotional and behavioral consequences. We tend to base our attempt to understand the past and make sense of today on that notion. The result of this $A = C$ approach, however, is a set of wrong conclusions about ourselves. I look at my past, for instance, and see occasional failures. I then pronounce myself a failure because of those events: I act according to the equation $A = C$. In doing this, I am letting events tell me who I am. Furthermore, because I assume that the events themselves determine my response, I see myself as unable to change unless events in my life change. Acting as if $A = C$ can cause us to feel doomed, forever connected to and controlled by the past.

Up to this point of the discussion, though, we have made a critical error. We've ignored our ABC's! And the letter *B* is crucial to a better understanding of ourselves and to a healthy letting go of the past. The letter *B* stands for our "Belief System," our thought patterns, and our self-talk. As stated in Chapter 1, it is these thoughts that cause and therefore can control our emotional and behavioral responses. Let's look at an example of how our thoughts (or belief system) can affect our responses to events in our lives.

Consider that an activating event in our lives is the fact that we are experiencing a wide range of emotions, most of which we don't understand. This event leads us to conclude (an emotional response) that we are out of control and abnormal. This response, however, is a false conclusion. The fact is that events and circumstances do not cause emotional and behavioral consequences. It is not *what* happens, but what we *think* about what happens to us that matters. We cannot alter the reality that at this moment our emotions seem uncontrollable. The determining factor, however, is not that reality, but what we think about that reality. Enter our belief system! It is telling us clearly that emotional turmoil is abnormal. When we listen to this message, we suffer the emotional consequence of feeling that we are out of control and abnormal.

If it is true that the key to escaping this negative consequence is found in our self-talk, then the challenge before us is to change our belief system. Where do we begin?

UNDERSTANDING SELF-TALK: THE KEY TO CHANGING OUR BELIEF SYSTEM

Our Thoughts Create Our Emotions

It is not the circumstances, but what we choose to think about the circumstances which will determine our emotional responses. It is not what "they" did to us, but what we think about those things that causes us to get angry. The battleground is in the mind; the battle cannot be fought against those other people.

Our Thoughts Affect Our Behavior

We will behave certain ways because of our self-talk. Consider, for example, these sentences:

"I can't forget what he/she did."
"Anytime we see each other, I lose control."
"He/she always makes me angry."

Consider, too, the story about a man who hitched a ride on a freight train. When his eyes became accustomed to the dark in the boxcar, he saw the word *Refrigerated* on the sides of the boxes. Believing those words but hoping to keep warm, he huddled in the corner as though to shut out the cold. The next day he was found dead. The temperature in the boxcar was in the 50s, but his self-talk must have convinced his body that it was freezing! In light of the story, look again at the three sentences listed above and imagine the behaviors that could result.

Our Perceived Center of Control Affects Our Behavior

Each of us has a center of control: it is that part of our minds that tells us what or who is in control of our lives and what or who owns us. Our behavior is determined by whatever thing or person we think is controlling our lives. Just as the person or thing which owns us gives us worth (Chapter 3), that same person or thing exercises control over our lives.

Numbers 13 offers us a good example of this phenomenon. Before the children of Israel finally entered Canaan, they sent an advance group of spies and explorers. They returned with the news that "all the people whom we saw . . . are men of great stature. . . . we were like grasshoppers in our own sight, and so we were in their sight" (Numbers 13:32–33). The scouts saw themselves as grasshoppers and the Canaanites as giants. This perception became their center of control and they behaved accordingly. Joshua's center of control, however, was God, so he confidently believed that, whatever the size of the Canaanites, Israel could still take the land.

Who or what is in control of your situation? Your ex? Your past? Your circumstances? God? In order to understand your own belief system, you need to answer that question for it is who owns you that determines your belief system.

We Often Think Irrationally

We choose (yes, choose) to think irrational thoughts about the actual events in our lives. We assume the worst too often and in doing so hand over the control of our minds and emotions to things, people, and events.

We Create Change in Our Lives by Gaining Control of Our Thoughts

As we struggle to change our thought patterns, the battleground is, naturally enough, our minds. We literally must fight against the irrational arguments and reasoning that take place in our minds. Paul exhorts us to "[bring] every thought into captivity to the obedience of Christ" (2 Cor. 10:5). Furthermore, if Christ is the One who owns us, if He is our Lord, then we can challenge and let go of any belief that is contrary to Christ's word about us.

The importance of Christ's word about us is dramatically illustrated in Luke's gospel. Jesus was dining with some religious leaders when He was approached by a woman who began to wash His feet with her hair.

Jesus' host thought to himself, "This man, if He were a prophet, would know who and what manner of woman this is who is touching Him, for she is a sinner." But Jesus knew his thoughts and let him know that the woman's kindness toward Him had been greater than that of His host. "I say to you, her sins, which are many, are forgiven, for she loved much" (see Luke 7:36–50).

With this pronouncement, Jesus gave the woman a new belief system about who she was and who she could become. As demonstrated by the diagram on page 95, Jesus continues to offer us a new belief system and a pronouncement of our value to Him.

We need to stop a minute. Many people misunderstand what is being said at this point. "Is this just another form of 'positive thinking'?" "Are you saying that we can change reality?"

A new belief system does not change reality. But it can change the way we perceive reality. Remember the Israelite spies mentioned earlier. The spies did not attempt to pretend that the giants didn't exist. They made a choice about who was in control.

Our new belief system is not a way of pretending that the

Old Belief System

A	B	C
(Activating Events)	(Belief System)	(Emotional and Behavioral Consequences)
My spouse left me.	Rejection determines worth and lovability.	I must be an unlovable person.
My emotions seem uncontrollable.	Emotional turmoil is abnormal.	I am personally out of control and abnormal.
My friends avoid me.	My worth as a friend depends upon my ability to earn love.	I need to earn the love of others.

New Belief System

My spouse left me.	God loves me regardless.	I *can* begin again.
My emotions seem uncontrollable.	Emotions are normal, natural, & neutral.	I *can* learn from these emotional signals.
My friends avoid me.	My "friends" do not determine my identity.	I *can learn to love* others without needing to perform because of dependency.

divorce, the pain, or the problems don't exist. It's more like looking at glass. We can focus on the glass and see only our reflections—with all the obstacles—or we can look through the glass to the heavens where we get a truer perspective of our problems and our lives. Giants and obstacles? Yes. Insurmountable? No.

Affirmation Exercise: My identity is always bigger than my past.

CONCLUSION

Adopting our new belief system is an act of faith because it will sometimes seem to contradict the way we feel or what we see. But faith is important because it demonstrates that we believe the God who owns us is faithful to carry out His plans for our wholeness. And He can do that only as we give Him control of our belief system. When we let Him be Lord or manager, He becomes the source of our identities. He tells us who we are, and that reality should be more powerful than anything in the world around us.

With time and effort, our new belief system can change the emotional and behavioral consequences in our lives. Notice that we did not say "change the *events* of our lives." We must remember that the events are not what is significant; rather, what we choose to believe about those events is what matters. Each one of us needs to be able to stop and reprogram his negative self-talk. We need to work on developing an awareness of these negative thoughts. Then we can work on forcing ourselves to stop thinking them! We could even say aloud, "Stop! Stop!" We might feel silly. We might be tempted to believe that this process won't work. And how easy it is to quit! But remember, this exercise is a beginning! It may even be helpful to write the new belief system on an index card and then read it every time negative thoughts occur to us. We can also write down any biblical passage which applies to our particular area of need. Remember, too, that to change, we can begin with just one small step. Let me give you a real-life success story.

Mary came to me one day with a concern of hers. She was to be taking part in the wedding of her daughter. Her ex-husband would, understandably, be attending. Mary's concern was legitimate: "How can I enjoy that event without being controlled by my anger toward him? I don't want to spend the whole day being uncomfortable! I know that my tendency is to remain tied to him and the past, but I want to begin to let go."

So we worked on Mary's belief system. During our time together, we isolated two thoughts for her to memorize: "I will lift up my eyes to the hills—/From whence comes my help?/My help comes from the LORD" (Ps. 121:1–2) and "You (referring to her ex-spouse) do not have the power to ruin my joy."

The wedding day came. This activating event could not be altered, but Mary's belief system had been transformed. She went through the day with the confidence that she was owned by her loving Father and mighty God. He was the source of her identity: she was no longer owned by her past.

She returned from the wedding with a smile from ear to ear. "It worked!" she exclaimed. "I can't change the past, but it doesn't need to have power over me!" I wholeheartedly agreed!

Letting go of the past is not

- something done in a vacuum,
- something we can only fantasize about,
- something that occurs overnight, or
- something that is easy.

But letting go of the past *is* possible! The activating events of the past can never be changed, but that doesn't matter. Our new belief system has put us in touch with a new center of control and that is the key to letting go. As we seek to move on from a failure or hurt in the past, we must answer the fundamental question "Who owns me?" When we come under the management of Jesus Christ, we realize that the past does not need to determine us. Freedom can't come by pretending that the past did not exist or by trying to amputate it from our lives. Listen to a story told by William Bridges.

Once there were two monks who were traveling through the countryside during the rainy season. Rounding a bend in the path, they found a muddy stream blocking their way. Beside it stood a lovely woman dressed in flowing robes.

"Here," said one of the monks to the woman, "let me carry you across the water." And he picked her up and carried her across. Setting her down on the farther bank, he went along in silence with his fellow monk to the abbey on the hill.

Later that evening the other monk said suddenly, "I think you made an error, picking up that woman back on our journey today. You know we are not supposed to have anything to do with women, and you held one close to you! You should not have done that."

"How strange," remarked the other. "I carried her only across the water. You are carrying her still."[2]

Chapter Eight

Loneliness: A Gift or a Curse?

*I*t's Friday night. You're alone and left to the task of entertaining yourself. You start with the TV. But news isn't exactly your idea of entertainment, so you move on to something else—leaving the TV on because the noise helps. What about something to eat? Please God, no more TV dinners! As you rummage through the refrigerator and cupboards, nothing is terribly appealing, so you settle for a pint of ice cream. "Oh well," you say, "I deserve it."

Having found something to eat, you move on to the stereo. That works fine. You sit listening to music and eating your ice cream to the beat of the song—until you hear it. It's "our song"! That does it. No more stereo! But now your mind is on that other person. Maybe TV is worth another try. No, you think you'll read a book. As the frustrating debate about what to do rages in your mind, you sit, almost motionless.

That's when it begins—the walls seem to be closing in around you. Needing to get out of the house, you throw on a coat and start to drive. You might end up at a movie, or going for more ice cream, or looking for a place to get a drink, or all three.

Loneliness. It happens to all of us. Married and single. Tall and short. Well-adjusted or neurotic. We all know plenty about loneliness. We know, for instance, that loneliness is not the same as aloneness. We know, too, that paradoxically loneliness can seize us most acutely when we're with other people. We know that this hollow sense of loneliness is an experience common to every human being. We know that loneliness is cited as the number one cause of premature death. But such knowledge is irrelevant when we are lonely.

We all know a lot about loneliness. Each of us can add some very personal, very specific definitions to this list. Loneliness is

- being single and aching to have someone share your life and love.
- assuming that those around you "have it all together" and look on you as being inferior.
- being married and unfulfilled.
- having a good day at work and then having only four walls to share it with.
- saying "I love you" when it's too late.
- having the feeling that no one would like you if you shared your innermost secrets.
- taking an inventory of your life and feeling like you made the wrong choices.
- hurting inside and realizing that no one seems to understand or care about your pain.[1]

I see us experiencing loneliness in four stages.

STAGE #1: Awareness

At one time or another, each of us becomes aware of a sense of isolation. Many of us attempt to postpone or even deny that awareness. We keep busy and are careful not to let on to those around us that deep inside we are crying tears of loneliness.

Our efforts to ignore the aching loneliness are futile. The time arrives when we are forced to look inward: we then acknowledge that we are lonely. We feel rejected; we feel separated from God and others. We sense the urgent need to wear masks—"I can't let others know how I really feel!" And we find ourselves prone to competition—"Maybe I could earn some respect and admiration."

At this point we need to remember what we said earlier in the book: it's okay to be where we are. It's okay to be at the awareness stage and it's important to be there. We may not like what we see as we look inside ourselves, but wisely, we will not have compounded the problems by hiding or repressing or denying the feelings that exist. We are honestly facing our genuine emotions.

Affirmation Exercise:	It is okay to be lonely. Loneliness is normal.

STAGE #2: Longing

On the heels of awareness comes the desperate longing to escape our loneliness. We long for love, for caring, for friendship. We want to be in a place where we can know others and be known by them: we desire that elusive thing called intimacy. We long for loneliness to disappear magically.

Into the middle of this tension comes the father of lies—the Bible calls him the "Deceiver"—and he tells a lie about loneliness. "Loneliness," Satan says, "is a solvable problem." And we swallow this lie hook, line, and sinker. We want to believe that loneliness can be solved and that it can be dealt with once and for all. That isn't how loneliness works, though. Loneliness is a normal human emotion which we will experience from time to time as long as we live.

At Stage #2, though, our powerful longing to be rid of our loneliness makes Satan's suggestion much more appealing than any high-sounding words about loneliness being an opportunity to learn about God or about ourselves. Desiring to leave our loneliness behind, we move on to . . .

STAGE #3: Fantasizing

If loneliness is solvable, all we need to do is find that key which will take away our loneliness forever! Relying on the two special phrases "when" and "if only," we imagine various solutions to our loneliness:

"When I get married . . ."
"When I'm successful . . ."
"If only my circumstances would change . . ."
"When my sex life improves . . ."

So we find ourselves going from one thing to the next, discarding each person or thing that does not (and cannot) remove our loneliness.

When nothing works, our loneliness causes us to turn inward even more. We think that once we "get our act together," we will be able to relate to and care for others. With this in mind, we relentlessly pursue any offer of a possible solution to our pain. These pursuits are encouraged by a society which thrives on exploiting our need for instant companionship. Commenting on clubs and organizations that are built on appeals for friendship and/or a mate, Lee Steiner observes, "Most of the advertising sent out by the clubs are masterpieces of double-talk, creating the impression that this is a guaranteed method of solving one's loneliness."[2]

Although this pursuit of a cure-all for our loneliness does not take away our loneliness, it does keep us occupied. And the guiding principle that loneliness is solvable encourages us to turn over any stone promising to give us the secret. In the end, however, we must face . . .

STAGE #4: The Breakdown of Our Fantasies

It doesn't take long before we realize that our games of "if only" and "when" do not magically remove our loneliness. Even so, many of us make such games a vocational hobby. We're afraid to acknowledge that loneliness is a part of each one of us and that it's okay to experience that loneliness.

When our fantasies finally do break down, anger follows close behind. It begins with a spirit of discontent. The anger may not be verbalized or even in our conscious minds, but the seed has been planted. We become aware of an apathetic or even cynical attitude toward other people and toward life in general. We find ourselves easily angered by circumstances ("I never seem to get a fair deal!"), by other people ("If I were in that person's place, life would be easier."), and by God ("He doesn't seem to answer, and anyway, I'm tired of asking."). We feel hurt and often become quite bitter. Our problem of loneliness has not yet been solved, and we are angry. Anger, however, only causes us to draw into our shells even further, and we end up cursing the very lives we long to enjoy.

THE GIFT OF LONELINESS

Having experienced the four stages of loneliness and finding ourselves still feeling painfully alone, we're frustrated and disappointed. And we can't help wondering what it would be like to have a world without loneliness.

Before we think too hard about that kind of world, I want you to think about something else. If God were going to give you a gift, what would you hope for? Happiness? Money? A mate? Would it surprise you if the gift He gave you were loneliness? That's right. Loneliness.

I believe loneliness actually is a gift from God. It is, therefore, not to be denied, run away from, or magically removed. Instead, loneliness is to be received and acknowledged as a gift and as an opportunity for personal awareness and growth.

As long as we see loneliness as a solvable problem, we cannot see it as a gift from God. When we can see loneliness as the gift from God that it truly is, we can grow, we can learn, and we can move on. How, then, do we begin to see loneliness as a gift?

We must first learn not to deny our loneliness; we must stop pretending that it doesn't exist. Our loneliness is real, and it is a normal part of life. Clark Moustakas explains:

> Loneliness is as much organic to human existence as the blood is to the heart. It is a dimension of human life whether existential, sociological, or psychological; whatever its derivatives or forms, whatever its history, it is a reality of life. Its fear, evasion, denial, and the accompanying attempts to escape the experience of being lonely will forever isolate the person from his own existence, will afflict and separate him from his own resources so that there is no development, no creative emergence, no growth in awareness, perceptiveness, sensitivity.[3]

I agree with that viewpoint and the Bible supports it. The Gospels suggest that even Jesus felt loneliness. Imagine, for example, His loneliness of not being understood by the close circle of disciples with whom He shared His life. At one point when Jesus predicted His death, the disciples "understood none of these things" (Luke 18:34). Later, after the agonizing cries to God in the Garden of Gethsemane, we sense Christ's feeling of abandonment. When he rose from praying, "He came to the disciples and found them asleep" (Matt. 26:40). Finally, there is Christ's haunting cry from the cross: "My God, My God, why have You forsaken Me?" (Mark 15:34). Our Lord knew loneliness and He faced it honestly.

Although we are free to turn to Jesus in our loneliness, we have a tendency to deny that loneliness. We want to live life independently, not leaning on other people or on God. We want to be in control and self-sufficient. "I can handle it!" we say, but a nagging sense of loneliness keeps getting in the way. Sometimes it becomes so severe that we can hardly think about anything else.

So how can loneliness be a gift?

I believe that God created us incomplete, not as a cruel trick to make us suffer, but as a means of moving us toward other people who have similar needs. This involvement with others is important, not as a solution to loneliness, but as the only possible context for real growth. As we said earlier, if we relate to others simply because they can take away our loneliness, they become objects we can easily discard.

Loneliness, that painful twinge inside that makes us reach out, is something for which we can be thankful. In Chapter 2, we talked about the importance of allowing other people to be part of the process of healing and growth. Growth can come only when we choose to give a little of ourselves away. Our temptation, however, is to withdraw and become isolated. Only because we become lonely do we reach outside our protective shells.

When we do reach out, we experience the mystery of God's love as it manifests itself in community. The irony is that this community of *agape* love is actually born in loneliness. Once we are in community as God intends us to be, we will see His image reflected in the way we relate to others. The characteristics of Christlikeness such as love, joy, or patience can only be reflected in relation to other people, not in isolation from them. When, because of our loneliness, we enter into the Christian community, we come to understand better God's plan and His love for us.

If we do not come to terms with our loneliness, we are, in the words of Henri Nouwen, like the "many people in this life [who] suffer because they are anxiously searching for the man or woman, the event or encounter, which will take their loneliness away." Nouwen goes on to give further definition to what we have been saying:

> The Christian way of life does not take away our loneliness; it protects and cherishes it as a precious gift. Sometimes it seems as if we do everything possible to avoid the painful confrontation with our basic human

loneliness, and allow ourselves to be trapped by false gods promising immediate satisfaction and quick relief. But perhaps the painful awareness of loneliness is an invitation to transcend our limitations and look beyond the boundaries of our existence. The awareness of loneliness might be a gift we must protect and guard, because our loneliness reveals to us an inner emptiness that can be destructive when misunderstood, but filled with promise for him who can tolerate its sweet pain.[4]

"But where is that 'promise' Nouwen speaks of?" we ask. "And how can I respond to my own sense of loneliness?"

To help you answer these questions and come to terms with your loneliness, I have two other questions for you to think about.

First, are you thankful for your loneliness?

Without a spirit of thankfulness, you will continue to try to avoid, at all costs, any lonely times. Consider, for a moment, how loneliness can have a positive effect on you. When you are lonely, you recognize your need for others. When you are lonely, you risk entering community. When you are lonely, you discover a family of brothers and sisters in Christ. If you didn't experience this loneliness, you would feel self-sufficient and self-reliant, and ironically, that would be the loneliest place of all. You would not enter into relationship with other people. You would not find a place of warmth, healing, and growth.

Still, thankfulness is difficult because you don't often *feel* thankful. That's when you need to recall Paul's description of Jesus in Hebrews 4:15–16:

> For we do not have a High Priest who cannot sympathize with our weaknesses, but was in all points tempted as we are, yet without sin. Let us therefore come boldly to the throne of grace, that we may obtain mercy and find grace to help in time of need.

Jesus knows our loneliness because He's been there. And Jesus knows the temptation to have the loneliness taken away by a quick fix. He's been there, too. And because He has experienced these same feelings, we can be confident of His understanding and love for us in our times of loneliness and need. We can also be thankful even when we don't feel thankful. Why? Because our confidence is based on what Jesus has done for us, not on what we feel. We can be confident in the hope that God knew what He was doing when He gave us the gift of loneliness. We can rest in the hope that God's gift is good.

The other question I want you to consider as you deal with your loneliness is this: even when all your feelings discourage this hope, how can you reach out?

When you focus on your need to remove your loneliness, you lose your ability to reach out to anyone else. Remember, though, that we said community is born of such loneliness. This means that loneliness

- is not to be denied,
- is not to cause self-pity, and
- is not solvable by a quick fix.

Instead, think of loneliness as a magnet. Let it draw you and other people together. In this respect, loneliness is a beautiful gift because without its pain some of us would wall ourselves in and remain locked in our separateness. The gift of loneliness gives us the desire and even the capacity to reach out. The pain we have experienced can then be a resource that allows us to be truly empathetic and compassionate with these people we meet. Hospitality, friendship, and community are therefore often born of pain and loneliness.

We have heard the Golden Rule often: "Do unto others as you would have them do unto you." Applied to the subject of loneliness, it could be restated this way: "Assume that everyone else in the world is at least as lonely as you are, and then act toward them as you would want them to act toward you." It is in reaching out that the pain of our loneliness becomes the "sweet pain" that Henri Nouwen mentioned earlier.

In this sweet pain of reaching out and giving a little of ourselves away, there is growth. In reaching out, there is hope. In reaching out, there is wholeness. The good news is that we don't have to reach out alone. There is Someone who stands with us: His name is Jesus. He lived, died, and lives again. While He lived, He reached out. He experienced loneliness, disappointment in His disciples, a sense of being abandoned by God, and the ultimate rejection of death on the cross. He lives again, though, to comfort and guide people who reach out to Him. He lives for you and me. Can we dare to reach out to Him? He is reaching out to us and He offers to be with us as we reach out to others.

————————Chapter Nine————————

Friendship

"*F*riends are the haven in the wilderness," Gail Sheehy
says, "even more so when a person is struggling for
bearings in the face of a life accident. It is simply
too hard to imagine confronting a normal passage or a major
setback all alone." In her book *Pathfinders,* Sheehy recounts a
story of friendship to which we can all relate.

Not wanting to ruin my weekend, Donna didn't tell me until Sunday
afternoon. We caught the last chair lift up the mountain. . . .
Our skis chattered over the ice until we came to the first stop. The sun
was low. The cold clamped around us. Shadows cut purple ruts into the
frozen mountain. Our silhouettes on the snow were sharp and definite.
"Leo and I are separating."
It came out clear as a smoke ring and as impossible for me to take in. I
asked her to repeat. . . .
She was trying to give me all the information as quickly and clearly as
possible in the hope that I could make some sense of it. She couldn't, she
said.
This was how it looked to me: the person closest to her in the world
had asked her to swallow a torch that had incinerated her tenderest parts.

It was scorching timber now, the foundation on which rested any idea at all of herself. Any moment there might be a shudder, a great implosion, and my dearest friend would cave in.

I told her the things she was. I tried to put some of the bricks back, one by one. "You're one of the most valuable people God ever made. I love you. I'm with you. If I can ever get these bloody skis turned around, I just want to hold you."

She later described how it looked to her: "There was nobody else on the mountain. It added to the feeling of isolation I'd had for a year. There we were, sharp outlines in all that white snow—but now it was two, instead of just one. I felt so close to you. When someone has rejected you so badly, you can't help thinking, 'I must be a worthless person.' But you said it wasn't true. And because you'd known me so long, I could believe you."[1]

All alone—the words have a terrifying ring to them. And yet, many of us choose to be all alone. Andrew Greeley says, "There are two kinds of loneliness that afflict human life. The first is the loneliness that comes from the human condition. It can be mitigated and alleviated but it cannot be eliminated. The other is the loneliness that we choose freely. It can always be conquered if we choose to do so."[2]

In the last chapter we spoke of loneliness as a gift from God. Too often, however, we don't see it as a gift and choose to fill our days with intense busyness or complete withdrawal so as to avoid facing our aloneness. Both choices are forms of isolation.

"But wait a minute," some of you may be contending. "Not all isolation is by choice. We may be in places where there are no friends. We have no one else to reach out to. Now where do we turn?"

That is a very real isolation. And I understand the fear of it. But we must not assume that, once isolated, we are destined to be isolated forever. We begin to see ourselves as victims of life and become resentful because we weren't dealt a fair hand by God. And we resent those around us because they never seem to reach out to us when we need them. So we stay isolated and afraid. And resentment—like a cancer—begins to eat away at us while we question whether or not life is worth living.

"But there's another isolation," say others of you who want to join our discussion. "What about the times I've reached out to others and have been disappointed or rejected?"

"Yes, that's right," still others have joined in. The conversation is starting to get interesting. "And what about the friends I had before my break-up? I counted on them when I was going through the turmoil and confusion. But as the tempest subsided, so did the phone calls, the invitations and the company."[3]

Friendship. It was hard enough when our lives were predictable and semi-sane. But now? Whom can we count on? Are friendships possible? Are they worth the risk? How do we build friendships? Must we "start from scratch"? Where do we go for community and support?

Good questions. All of them. But before we begin to work our way through them, let's take a minute and remind ourselves why friendships and support are essential to begin with. What is a friend? I define *friend* as "someone who creates an environment where one can be nurtured and who allows one to create an environment for one's self to be nurtured in return."

Why do we need friends?

1. *Friends lead us away from isolation.*

John Donne was right: "No man is an island." C. S. Lewis said it another way: "No one can paddle his own canoe."

Isolation is a killer. In isolation we lose our sense of balance. We lose perspective. The only eyes through which we can view the world are our own. And through our eyes, we are tempted to give in to unnecessary discouragement and self-pity. Friends are God's gift to remind us that the world is bigger than our worries and problems.

2. *Friends encourage the best in us.*

Friends require risk. By nature we want to stay comfortable. And in our pain, very little motivates us to care or give or risk. We may want to change, but we're not sure we're willing to take the risk involved. It means letting others know us—in our pain and confusion. It means letting others help us succeed—even though we don't think we deserve it. It means letting some be our friends—even though we're afraid to let anyone close.

I can honestly say that if it weren't for my friends, I wouldn't be writing this book today. They wouldn't let me give up on myself. They wouldn't let me "throw in the towel." They demanded the best from me, and you can bet I put up a fight. I didn't want people demanding my best. I wanted to quit. In hindsight, I'm glad now that I didn't. I'm glad for friends.

3. *Friends create for us community and family.*

In an article on coping with disaster, the *Los Angeles Times* asked the following question, "Why are some disaster survivors more resistant to psychological problems than others?" Their answer? Top on the list was "support systems. Survivors with strong support systems—families, friends, etc.—seem to do better. 'Support systems are absolutely critical,' psychologist Calvin J. Fredrick said. 'People who are isolated will have the most difficult time adjusting.'"[4]

Unfortunately for many of us, our natural families have refused to support us in our pain. Our "family" must be our friends. Ideally, we find them in the church, but there are many horror stories to the contrary. It's been said that the church is the only organization that "shoots its wounded." Too true. But let's not give up hope. Maybe we can begin to make a difference in reversing that trend. It's just too easy to blame all our relational difficulties on the church.

4. *Friends allow us the opportunity not only to receive, but to give.*

Because of the turmoil and understandable insecurity we're experiencing, we're convinced we have nothing to offer anyone. We assume we can only receive from others—and even that is difficult to do.

We said earlier that the quickest road to wholeness is through giving a little of ourselves away. The temptation, of course, is to believe that giving is measured only in quantity. That's not true. Giving is an attitude of the heart. It says that "regardless of what

I have to give you, I want to make sure you know we're in this together."

5. *Friends make forgiveness real.*

Forgiveness says, "You don't need to perform or prove anything to me. I don't accept you based on what you owe me."

I discovered that in my beginning-again process, I wanted accomplices, not friends. I wanted people around me who would confirm my suspicions, applaud my need to be the victim, listen to my tales of woe. The pay-off for me was the fact that such people reinforced my bondage. I stayed tied to my past, to my need to make things fair and balance the scales, to my need to be vindicated.

But true friends took the courage to challenge me to accept and give forgiveness. They were willing to ask, "Terry, how are you really feeling?"—and they meant it. They really wanted to know. So I began to answer such questions. Slowly at first. "Gentle risking," I call it. But it was the necessary step to become real and to be really forgiven.

TO GAIN A FRIEND, YOU MUST BE A FRIEND.

My need to be a victim infiltrated all areas of my life. I wanted friendship, but I wanted someone else to do all the work. "When you reach out to me, I'll be glad to reciprocate and be your friend." But friendship doesn't work that way. Most everyone else seemed just as cautious as I was.

I learned that friends attract friends. What does that mean? It means I had to choose to be a friend, to be kind and open and willing to give. With anyone? Of course not. I realized that if I wanted to be friends with everyone, I'd be friends with no one. But I knew I had to stop worrying about me, and wondering if anyone cared, to see other hurting people around me who were also looking for friends.

> **Affirmation Exercise:** Friendship begins with me.

Have you ever wondered why we tend to marry people just like our former spouses? It's because all of us have antennas that attract certain kinds of people into our lives. As long as we assume we're victims, we'll continue to be confused and frustrated by repeating the same relational problems.

To understand relationships, we need to take a look at our "antennas." What kinds of people do we attract? Bitter people attract bitter friends. Negative people attract negative friends. We attract people who reinforce our weaknesses.

Let's stop a minute and take an inventory. What kind of people do you attract?

Pain doesn't cancel friendships. I lived with the assumption that I had to wait for all my pain to disappear before I could begin to develop any significant friendships. I was wrong. In fact, if you are waiting for your pain to completely "go away," you will be waiting forever. Instead you will resort to repression and attempt to convince yourself that you're over your pain. Oh yes, it's true that much of your pain will lose its power over you. But that doesn't mean you will ever lead a pain-free existence.

Facing pain is never easy. But we must learn to see it as a signal that friendship—giving and receiving—is possible. Pain and vulnerability are the fertile ground for the development of true intimacy. That may sound hard or unrealistic—or even foolish; I'm not saying we should subject ourselves to pain simply for its rewards. But I am saying that we can be realistic about pain. Pain is inevitable. Misery is our option.

If pain is inevitable, then we no longer need to run from it. We can learn from it. We can take small steps of growth and friendship without needing to pretend that "I've got my act together."

In fact, sensitivity to our own pain makes us sensitive to the pain of those around us—and that makes us better friends. I had always assumed that none of the people around me were plagued by the insecurities, hurts, and frustration I was experiencing. I've since discovered how wrong that assumption was.

We are all incomplete people in a broken world, and no one of us can make it alone. Friendship doesn't wait to begin with perfect people. It is the bond that makes life real in an imperfect world.

SUPPORT GROUPS

In a world of change and vulnerability, the friendships from a support group are vital. Are you in a support group? Do you know of any friends in a support group? Are there any groups available in your area?

How do support groups begin? Maybe you can begin one. Support groups are gatherings of between three and twelve people on a regular basis for the purpose of nurture and support. They're necessary for several reasons.

Support groups are intentional. In support groups, we intend to face our relationships. We intend to look at our fears and the obstacles to our growth. Meeting with support groups reminds us that we have chosen to begin again.

Support groups fight isolation. When isolated, we lose proper perspective of our situation; we tend to overestimate the power of our pain, and we easily fall prey to ill-advised decisions. Support groups give us a context for facing life, a context that's bigger than our fears.

Support groups provide affirmation. Nothing facilitates growth better than a compliment or a note of affirmation. At a time when criticism seems endless—from the ex, from friends, from the family, from the kids—an oasis of affirmation is essential to our health.

Support groups provide focus. When we isolate ourselves, we can easily convince ourselves that our perspective is the right perspective on all our problems. Unfortunately, that's not so. Although we don't necessarily enjoy being told we're wrong, what a relief it is to be able to focus on the real issues.

After a lecture on beginning again, one man said to me, "I

agree with everything but the fact of same-sex friendships. Where do you find people like that? You must be rare to have had good friends." Perhaps I was lucky. I wish there were five easy steps to friendship. But there aren't; finding and developing friendships isn't easy. But it is essential. So I must leave with you a note of encouragement that regardless of your reservations or insecurities or pain, friends are worth the risk. Start slowly. Take gentle risks. Remember, where you arrive isn't what counts, it's the journey that's important.

Chapter Ten

Relating to an Ex-Spouse

A s she sat in my office, one young woman stated the issue very succinctly: "A divorce is a lot like a death, except in divorce, the 'corpse' is still walking around. And how am I supposed to relate to him?"

We have a great temptation in divorce recovery to spend all our energy trying to understand the behavior of our ex-spouses ("Why did this happen?" or "How could he/she do that?"). This is a battle we are destined to lose. Why? Because the battleground is in our minds and as a result any battle will only hurt us. Until we realize the self-destructive nature of any attempt to understand our ex-spouses' behavior, the concepts in this chapter can have little or no effect on our lives. As a means of determining how close we are to being able to leave behind the impossible project of trying to understand their actions, let's look at six myths that may influence how we deal with our ex-spouses.

MYTH #1:

"If only I could cut my heart out . . .
    I could relate to him/her more objectively."
    I could make sensible decisions."
    I could cope better with my life."

This myth assumes that our emotions—especially the painful sense of loss and rejection—cloud our ability to deal with reality. In part, that is true. But the reality is this: cutting our hearts out would not alleviate the pain; it would only deepen it. In his book *The Four Loves,* C. S. Lewis richly articulates some profound truths about love:

> To love at all is to be vulnerable. Love anything, and your heart will certainly be wrung and possibly be broken. If you want to make sure of keeping it intact, you must give your heart to no one, not even to an animal. Wrap it carefully around with hobbies and little luxuries; avoid all entanglements; lock it up safe in the casket or coffin of your selfishness. But in that casket—safe, dark, motionless, airless—it will change. It will not be broken; it will become unbreakable, impenetrable, irredeemable. The alternative to tragedy, or at least to the risk of tragedy, is damnation. The only place outside Heaven where you can be perfectly safe from all the dangers and perturbations of love is Hell.[1]

Love does hurt, and at this point after our relationships have ended, our emotions are simply signaling to us that we have hurts that need to heal. These signals are necessary and they are normal. They ask us to look at larger questions about ourselves, our relationship to God, and our way of being in relationships with other people. If we could cut our hearts out and look at our ex-spouses more objectively, then we would be avoiding any and all of the deep questions we must deal with if healing is to take place.

MYTH #2:

"If only I knew the reason why the relationship ended . . .
    I could understand."

it wouldn't hurt as much."
it would ease my mind and take less emotional energy."

This myth suggests that understanding alleviates pain. Although we all would like to have answers to the question "Why?" such understanding would have absolutely no bearing on the healing process. Knowing the reasons why our relationships ended or why our partners did what they did (if a clear reason even exists!) will not speed up the healing process or remove one bit of the hurt. Still, wanting to understand, we walk down a path we hope will lead either to a guarantee that this hurt will never happen to us again or to a scapegoat we can blame, thereby removing from ourselves the responsibility of needing to change.

While collecting various explanations in hopes of finding a guarantee, we tend never really to believe the stories anyway. Instead, we hope to hear another, more convincing account on down the line. Having failed to discover a believable or acceptable explanation, we are no closer to this guarantee that we will never again be involved in painful relationships. If we choose the second option and hope to discover a scapegoat, we latch on to any and every feasible explanation that might relieve us from our role and responsibility. And we will be failing to deal honestly with the situation.

What's important, however, is not what happened or why it happened, but what we believe about what happened. This myth of "If only I knew . . ." does not encourage us to look at our thought processes: it encourages instead an unhealthy and narrow focus on the past. And this focus on the past and on what the other people did to cause our relationships to end keeps us from looking at and learning about ourselves.

MYTH #3:

"If only I knew what's wrong with me . . .
   I would know why there was failure."

I could more easily cope with the pain, knowing
that whatever is wrong with me caused the problem."

This myth lets us use ourselves as the scapegoat for the divorce. As long as we're blaming someone or something (even ourselves), we're still avoiding responsibility. Feeling victimized, we come to replace responsibility with self-pity, and self-pity keeps us from having to make any changes in our lives. Self-pity says, "Please feel sorry for me because I'm not capable of changing and moving on. I need you to reinforce my inability to grow and to take responsibility for myself." Self-pity inevitably short-circuits recovery.

MYTH #4:

"If only my ex would suffer as much as I do . . .
the situation would seem fairer."
I could accept my hurt."

This myth fits with a major assumption in most divorces: "My ex is always better off than I am." Due to that person's methods of coping (which may be quite different from yours), he or she seems to suffer less, to pay less in terms of the consequences, and to avoid most of the emotional struggles and pain.

There remains one important but unanswered question: does it matter how well the other person is doing? Even if it is true that he or she is coping well (and it is not), does it really matter to your healing process?

It matters only because we want fairness: we want our ex-es to suffer as we are suffering. But what happens to them has no real impact on us; what we believe about them, however, will affect us. In other words, what we believe about what happens matters more than the events themselves. The idea of fairness and equal suffering actually has no bearing on either our healing or on our relationships with our ex-spouses.

One other note. As long as we believe the myth that the other person isn't hurting, we will continue to wish that he or she will suffer. We will remain enslaved to our past and to our need to get even.

MYTH #5:

"If only I could talk about it enough . . .
     it would all make sense."
     the pain would diminish."

This myth proposes that telling our stories over and over again takes away the pain and hurt of a divorce. Up to a point, this is true. Verbal acknowledgment allows us to be honest and open about where we stand and about the need to move on. Continued verbal acknowledgment, however, can be a mask behind which we hide. Rather than moving forward, we continue to bask in self-pity, to play the blame game, and to strive to justify our pain. ("After all, he/she was so bad to me that I can afford to wallow in the agony for a few years.")

There is a definite difference between telling one's story in a continual rehash of external facts (this is not beneficial) and talking about emotions as a means of eventually assuming responsibility for what's inside. This release of emotions is beneficial for the honest acknowledgment of where we are, the important first step toward growth.

MYTH #6:

"If only I had another chance . . .
     I would make it right."
     I wouldn't have to go through this hellish experience."

First, we need to consider honestly why we want another chance. Do we just want to prove to our ex-spouses that we're more okay than they think we are? Or do we genuinely want a reconciliation?"

We aren't saying that the desire to try to restore the relationship is wrong. Reconciliation is always the first option. But, after a point, this myth tends toward rationalization, blame, and self-pity.

This myth can create false hope. And such false hope can be destructive if it keeps us from dealing honestly with the reality of the present hurt. Hoping to alleviate the painful realization that our past is irreversible, we're tempted to play "things I wish I had said" games. Again, these games only serve to deepen our wounds; they do not bring healing.

Each of the above six myths affects our center of control. When and if we believe any one of them, we give away our power to change, to repent, to grow, and to move on. We place our hope in someone or something other than God, and that thing or person becomes our center of control.

Affirmation Exercise:	I am no longer married to my ex-spouse.
	I will relate to (name your ex-spouse) in a different way.

RELATING TO MY EX-SPOUSE

Having examined the myths about relating to our ex-spouses, we can now consider the difficult task of trying to establish healthy working relationships with them. As one woman in my office put it so matter-of-factly, "This divorce would be a lot easier if my ex weren't involved!"

Her remark was understandable and our tendency to be affected by our ex-mates is predictable. To break the link that leaves us controlled by our past relationships and paralyzed when it comes to dealing with our ex-spouses in any positive way, let's consider the following six guidelines.[2]

Make the Break as Clean as Possible

Many of us don't know how to "quit our marriages." We hang on to relationships which no longer exist, and by hanging on we are saying, "I choose to give this nonexistent relationship power over my life and identity." This unhealthy dependence only serves to short-circuit the process of getting to know ourselves and understanding where we can grow and move on.

This clean break should not be violated in the name of love. Initially, we don't need to be martyrs for love: "I want him/her happy, whatever that means about our relationship and however much that hurts me." We may, however, insist that we still truly love our ex-partners and therefore cannot break away completely. If we really love them, though, we will want what is best for them and for ourselves. What is best for each of us can come only as we take responsibility for ourselves. Our prolonged dependence on relationships which no longer exist does not allow that responsibility to develop and therefore cannot be genuine love. As difficult as it may sound, only a clean break can serve love. It starts with love for ourselves; it becomes love for our ex-spouses. Consider the fact that loving behavior avoids unhealthy confrontations and lets go of broken relationships.

Furthermore, a clean break helps both parties of a divorce redefine their individual identities after they have been involved in a nonnurturing relationship. The clean break gives them both the opportunity to understand themselves. Once that happens, they can redefine the relationship with the other person: "She is the mother of my children" or "He is part of the past." In this newly defined relationship, neither person's identity is wrapped up in the other person.

Carol's case reinforces the assertion that only a clean break can serve love. Because she needed help with household repairs and the lawn, she had her ex-husband come over at least once a week. In return for his help, she fixed him dinner. This had been going on for ten years since their divorce! Finally she confessed, "I was waiting for the day when he would walk in and it would be like 'old times' again." Carol assumed that she was acting out of love. In fact, she was continuing to live out a fantasy—and she had willingly sacrificed her own identity and freedom to that dream. She still considered herself Don's wife: she had refused to make a clean and healthy break from the past.

Live One Day at a Time

The process of letting go of the past and of coming to understand the relationship to an ex-spouse is not an easy one. We will often be tempted to give up the fight. Jim Smoke reminds us that problems are solved and plans are made one day at a time. Similarly, we learn to deal with our ex-spouses one day at a time. Wishing and worrying about things of the past or the future will do nothing to speed up or avoid the process of learning to relate to them in a healthy manner.

We may also be concerned about things other than how to deal with our ex-spouses and these worries can be further roadblocks to healing. Consider your five most pressing worries. Write them down and then answer these questions:

- How many of the worries pertain to today?
- How many worries can I do anything about?
- How many of the things I listed are actually my responsibility?
- What can I do about these worries today?

Also, take comfort from the words of the apostle Paul. Philippians 4:6–7 says:

> Be anxious for nothing, but in everything by prayer and supplication, with thanksgiving, let your requests be made known to God; and the peace of God, which surpasses all understanding, will guard your hearts and minds through Christ Jesus.

When I was learning to live one day at a time, I suddenly

realized that most of my thoughts about my ex-spouse dealt with the past or the future. But each one of us has only been given today. Knowing that, we can choose to focus our self-talk on the responsibilities of today. No longer do we need to give away the controls of our lives to our ex-spouses or to our past or to anything or anyone else.

Living in today is difficult. We think we're not as far along as we should be. "If only yesterday had been different today would be easier." Or, "I'll have better opportunities for growth next month." Or, "There isn't anyone to help me face today." But if God meant it when He said He loves us for no good reason, then that changes the way we view today. How does that happen? Slowly. One day at a time.

Give Up the Need to Understand Behaviors

As we've said before, our desire and efforts to understand what happened will not hasten the healing process. On the contrary, they can only serve to keep us locked into the past as we look backward for the reasons for the hurt.

Why do we want to understand anyway? In order to convince ourselves that the blame and the pain have been equally distributed? In order to place blame on someone other than ourselves? If we blame things and people around us, we may be doing so in hopes that people will understand why we are the way we are. They will see that there is really nothing wrong with us!

As we've said, though, our need to understand makes us a slave to our past and does not allow us the possibility of relating to our ex-spouses in a nonjudgmental way. We will lose the ability to see them as individuals: we will be focused on what those people have done.

Quit Accepting Responsibility for Your Ex-Spouse

As long as we continue to accept responsibility for our ex-mates we take our eyes off ourselves and our need to change.

This responsibility can take one of two forms.

1. We can feel responsible for rescuing our ex-spouses. We'll wonder how they can survive without us. We'll need to feel needed; we'll want to know that we're important and necessary.

Some time had passed since my separation. I remember secretly wishing that my wife would fall apart without me. But such did not happen. In fact, when I did see her, she was doing well. What a blow to my ego!

Why did I react that way? Because I had tied my identity into my need to rescue my ex-wife. In reality, then, she still controlled me. She still told me who I was. And I continued to buy into that game. Eventually I chose to move on from that kind of situation. My identity ceased to be dependent upon my ex-wife or my need to be there for her. My identity became based instead on my status as a child of God.

2. We can feel responsible for justifying—or at least rationalizing—our ex-spouses' behavior.

After a divorce there is a strong temptation to wonder about everything your ex-spouse does. Where is she going? Who is he dating? Why wasn't he home? Sometimes we use the children to spy for us. Or we work with a network of people who can give us the latest information about what is going on in his/her life.

The thinking is this: if I can know what he/she is doing now, I can deal with this pain because I feel as if I have control. "Control of what?" becomes the question. Again, the reality is that we're still seeking our worth from nonexistent relationships: we allow something from the past to consume both us and our future.

We need to see that whatever we assume responsibility for can own us. It can have power over our identity and keep us from growing and moving on. When we accept this truth, we can begin the process of change. We can let our self-talk take on a new focus. We can let it point us to those things for which we really are responsible and away from those things for which we are not responsible.

One final note. Because of our need to take responsibility for our ex-es, we may have difficulty expressing our anger toward them. As one woman said, "How can I call him a jackass? That reflects badly on me. After all, I lived with that jackass for ten years!" She was still unable to separate herself from her ex-spouse. She was taking on the responsibility of making him look okay in everyone's eyes because she felt that only then would she look okay. Consequently she repressed her true feelings and was unable to be honest with herself and others. Are you allowing your ex to be this kind of barrier to change and growth? Consider, too, what you can do this week to grow and more clearly establish your own identity.

Don't Let Your Children's Behavior Intimidate You

The feelings and actions of our children can be definite stumbling blocks in our efforts to establish healthy relationships with our ex-spouses. There are a couple of reasons for this.

First, most children want their parents to get back together. Seeing that desire expressed causes us to be tempted by false hope, but any attempt at reconciliation apart from the mutual commitment of both us and our ex-spouses cannot be the basis for healthy relationships. On the contrary, such reasons as "we did it for the children" can keep us from dealing with the real issues which caused the hurt in the beginning.

There are also the many questions by our children which can inflict a burden of guilt. We hear them ask, "Where's Mommy?"; "Why did you make Daddy move away?"; and "Is it my fault that Mommy doesn't live here anymore?" When we hear those questions we must let our self-talk remind us that our children's hurt does not have the power to tell us who we are; our children's hurt cannot tell us that we are bad and should feel guilty. We are quite able to address their needs and questions without having to justify, rationalize, blame, or please.

Avoid Being Consumed by Pettiness

We are usually surprised to find that in our attempts to relate to our ex-spouses, we revert to childish behaviors and pettiness. We vacillate between love and hatred. We threaten to get even. We throw tantrums, tell lies, and exhibit various jealous and passive-aggressive behaviors.

We may pause long enough in the midst of all this to shout, "I'm not really like this! But he/she makes me act this way!" You know these scenes. They're replayed often as we sort through our broken relationships. We feel like children when we behave this way and we don't like it—but we continually find ourselves falling into the pattern.

How do we avoid this pettiness? Again, the battleground is our minds and therefore the war must be waged by means of self-talk. In relation to our ex-spouses, then, it's time for disarmament—and this won't necessarily be mutual. It must, however, be unilateral. Even if they want to fight, we can choose not to give them any ammunition! Gail Sheehy says we have a real reason for prolonging these battles. What is the point, one wonders, in wasting more years listlessly tossing bombs in a war that is over? Why can't she just get on with her own expansion? The same reason comes up so often. If she loses him as the enemy on whom she can blame all her troubles, then she must realize that the enemy is inside. So long as this possibility remains unacceptable, she will continue to battle with a phantom villain.[3]

Our self-talk can affirm the fact that our ex-partners do not own us and that we're not obligated to let them push our buttons. This may mean saying no to a dinner invitation, so we can "stay friends." It may mean saying, "It's not healthy for me to keep talking to you," and hanging up the telephone. It may mean the need to stop asking mutual friends, "How's she/he doing without me?"

Easy? No. Necessary? Yes.

CONCLUSION

Having acknowledged the difficult aspects of establishing a healthy relationship with an ex-spouse, we have begun the process of change and of growth. We have acknowledged where we are as well as our capacity to move on. We have realized that

- we can make a clean break.
- we can choose to live one day at a time.
- we can give up our need to understand.
- we can give up responsibility for our ex-spouses.
- we can refuse to allow the children's behavior to intimidate us.
- we can avoid pettiness.

No matter how much or how little interaction we have with our ex-spouses, we can have healthy relationships with them. Since they no longer control us and we are not responsible for them, we can begin to be responsible for ourselves. When one day we notice our self-talk has been about our actual responsibilities and needs, we can realize that we are truly beginning again.

———————— Chapter Eleven ————————

Sex: Another Battleground

I had grasped the principles of letting go. I now believed I stood forgiven and that I was on my way to forgiving others. Without realizing it, however, I was driven to immediate relationships, believing that I had "recovered" and not thinking that I was using the new relationships as a padding against reality.

I was single again. And dealing with my sexuality was not easy for me. I was confused and lonely, and I wanted someone to love me. I had hoped I could move on with my life without dealing with (or seriously looking at) the subject of my body or my sexuality. Somehow I separated myself from my body. I didn't realize how closely tied my person is to my sexuality. What was the result? The games I played in my mind had consequences in my body and those consequences did not lead to recovery. Instead they locked me into old behavior patterns, dependencies, fears, and the need for denial.

Consciously or subconsciously, many of us enter relationships and write checks with our bodies in the same way that others use repression or withdrawal to avoid painful reality. To assume that we can walk through the beginning-again process in a bodyless state is silly. The reality is that God created us as "body persons." Author Don Nicholl explains this well:

> For what we do with our bodies, what we put into them, what we make of them, these are spiritual tasks which we are called to carry out in the name of holiness. There is no division in reality between the material and the spiritual; our spirituality is manifested by our treatment of matter.[1]

We need, therefore, to take into account the impact our sexuality has on our emotional and spiritual health. That was something I didn't want to face, because I felt most vulnerable and unsure sexually. I had the unsettling feeling that God was waiting to "catch me" doing something wrong.

Affirmation Exercise:	What I repress owns me. It is okay for me to be honest about my sexuality.

If the activating events in our lives include sexuality—and they do—and if our thoughts determine our behavior, then we need to understand the thoughts and consequences of our behavior. To do so, we must begin with a re-education in the area of theology.

1. *We were created by God as "body persons."* The consequence is that our sexuality—our maleness and femaleness, our sexual urges, our capacity to relate to one another physically—is part and parcel of creation. As part of God's creation, sexuality received the divine okay: God said, "It is good." That was important for me to hear because I had been raised on the idea that if it felt good (or had to do with the body), it was wrong. Instead of having a healthy understanding of my body, I was repressing my sexuality, thinking that such repression was spiritual. Once I understood that sexuality is a gift of God, I began to bring my sexual thoughts and feelings to the conscious level. Then I was

free to make conscious choices—either appropriate or inappropriate ones. But as long as my desires were repressed, I was making choices by default. I was reacting, not choosing.

2. *Sex does not exist as an end unto itself.* Rather, if we have a biblical understanding of sexuality we realize that sex is part of a process toward intimacy. Andrew Greeley observed that "every sexual act has a propensity toward permanence."[2]

You and I were created as intimate beings who can find fulfillment within covenantal relationships, that condition of knowing and being known, that state of vulnerability and complete honesty, that awareness of being fully alive. For us to be healthy, our sexual behavior must correspond to our levels of covenantal commitment. It is not surprising to find intercourse reserved for marriage. The vulnerability expressed in intercourse requires a covenant that can "back up" such a commitment. Intercourse outside that bond of commitment can be a stumbling block to intimacy, actually preventing that which we desire.

3. *Sexuality is not a "tamable" force.* In other words, it is never completely understood. We have desires we don't understand and must not feel confused and guilty about them. I was glad to realize I don't have to "know all the answers" or "have my act together." Once again, the journey is what matters, not the point of arrival. Andrew Greeley put it this way:

> . . . not that the taming of sexuality is an appropriate goal, for a tame sexuality is not a human sexuality—and probably one that is not much fun either. To argue, as I have in these pages, that sexuality is a raw, elemental force is not to say that one should be ashamed of primitive passion, much less try to tame it. The argument, rather, is that the beginning of sexual wisdom is to understand that we are dealing with a power that cannot be tamed. Living with sexuality does not mean eliminating its primal force; it means, rather, understanding how primal the force is and channeling it in directions which are both socially and personally productive."[3]

To deny the struggle is to forfeit the journey.

4. *God desires what is best for us.* He wants us healthy. He wants us fully alive, and He wants us whole. God is "pro-life."

This word needs to be rescued from the narrow confines of the abortion issue. Pro-life means just that—"for life." We have been created with the capacity to understand and enjoy life to its fullest. Unfortunately, most of our decisions and behaviors lead us away from such fullness of life. In fact, they lead us to frustration, anxiety, and tension. They lead us from life toward inner death.

I needed to change my view of God. I had always assumed that as far as my sexuality was concerned God was "on the other team." He was waiting from His heavenly perch with a hammer to keep me in line. To believe that "God is for me" was a new thought. I began to understand God's plan for me is fullness of life through Him. "I have come that they may have life, and that they may have it more abundantly" (John 10:10). I was not surprised, then, to find His great concern for my ethical life.

God is concerned that our choices produce life in us. Whether or not those choices are easy is beside the point. In fact, I can assure you that dealing with our sexuality is *not* easy. It's difficult to decide on the basis of fullness of life.

What do pro-life decisions bring us?

- peace of mind
- completeness
- an environment of nurturing
- joy
- wholeness
- selflessness
- good mental and physical health

5. *Out of its proper context, sexuality can lead to emotional and spiritual death.* Our decisions can get in the way of God's best interest for us. Our bad choices will keep us from being whole and alive. Unhealthy choices will produce:

- discomfort
- calloused emotions

133

- disillusionment
- self-centeredness
- ineffectiveness
- incompleteness
- dissatisfaction

Once we realize the consequences of our improper sexual behavior, we no longer have to be controlled by a list of do's and don't's.

Although we may agree about these five assumptions, we must still face an issue more real to us than any theory of sexuality: how can we make wise sexual decisions in a context of loneliness, insecurity, and high social pressure ("Everybody's doing it!")? Where do we turn for answers? Should we ignore our sexual urges and deny our sexuality?

As a single adult, I longed for the ability, first, to make a clean, clear decision in favor of God's ideal and, second, to learn to be happy with that decision—a step which is even more difficult! The fact remained, however, that amidst the myriad of emotions, conflicts, and pressures, I allowed myself to get caught up in games which carried me along until I cried, "Stop! This ride is taking me nowhere!" Yes, because the realities seemed intense and overpowering, I passively attended to my need to be close to someone, my need to be needed, and my need to be "loved."

What I really needed, though, was a place where I could be honest about myself and my sexuality. I needed to confront the issue of my sexuality. I needed to recognize my loneliness and sense of need, my failure and the resulting guilt, my hope for and the possibility of growth.

To begin that process, I had to be honest about where I was (the same step we discussed in Chapters 2 and 3 as being foundational for any movement toward recovery). I had to be honest about myself and about the games I so skillfully played. Such honesty was not for the purpose of morbid introspection; it was for the purpose of acknowledging where I was. Until I faced where I was, I tended to feel that I was unable to move on. Believing, however, that God does want what is best for me, I began the difficult but important process of trying to be honest about myself and my body.

What are the games that we are so prone to play and that get in the way of dealing with our sexuality in a healthy way?

SEXUAL GAMES

We Assume We're Exempt from the Classic Rebound Relationship

This assumption keeps our defenses down and before we know it we're emotionally and physically involved with others. We are then apt to experience either a sense of guilt or sense of relief.

First, we may feel guilty for being weak enough to fall into a rebound relationship. Ironically, this sense of guilt immobilizes us and makes it difficult to end what we know to be unhealthy relationships. We also worry about feeling even guiltier if we hurt the other people we leave. We can find it easier to stay in bad situations and avoid hurting other people. We want to feel good about ourselves—we don't want to hurt anyone—so we stay in bad relationships and hurt ourselves, if not the other people as well. We live according to the words of one woman who said, "At least bad love is better than no love."

If we don't feel guilty in these relationships we may instead experience a sense of relief. We are finally feeling important or worthy or interesting again. We can be so relieved and entranced by the fact that we're being loved that we give little or no thought to the health or rightness of the relationships.

Both of these responses—of feeling guilty or relieved—are unhealthy and can only be prevented by an honest awareness of

Beginning Again

our potential weakness and of the fact that we are not exempt
from the possibility of a rebound relationship.

We Focus Continually on Our Sexual Needs

Ironically, focusing on the problem only magnifies it, trigger-
ing a vicious cycle which requires us to meet our sexual needs,
whatever the cost. Consider, for example, what happens when
you are dieting and someone shows you a big bowl of ice cream
and then tells you not to think about it. The thought of that
food consumes you, and any thought of good health or the goal
of losing weight goes out the window.

Similarly, we know that to fight the sexual urge directly is to
lose the battle. Why? Because in trying to do so, we give such
needs our complete attention. By continually focusing on our
sexual needs, we give those needs the authority to control us. In
effect, our sexual needs tell us who we are as they consume our
energy, our thoughts, our time—as they consume all of us.

We Become Manipulative in Our Relationships

If we're afraid to stop and admit our sexual weakness, we find
that our sexual needs themselves actually control us and that we
will stop at nothing to meet those needs. People become mere
objects to us as we attempt to satisfy our needs. We find our
relationships characterized by "steak-dates": if we give something in exchange for sex, the trade justifies the sex. As one man
matter-of-factly said to a woman, "The dinner is on me; the
night is on you." There are no faces involved in this game, only
bodies.

We Give in and Then Feel Guilty

Being pulled in these opposite directions, we play the game
"By no means!/Maybe . . ." and shift the responsibility to the
other person. "After all, I didn't say yes," we argue, hoping to

136

convince ourselves that we were helpless victims. By telling ourselves that we didn't actually say yes, we avoid responsibility for our actions. This reasoning, of course, is flimsy. Thinking this way only serves to compound the problem by leading us to repress real feelings. The result is a building resentment that we harbor against all those who "take advantage" of us.

We Avoid a Conscious Choice

This is a comfortable game because it keeps us from having to assume any responsibility. "Let whatever happens, happen," we say, wanting to avoid choices we don't really want to make. Ignoring the need to choose does not remove the consequences. Furthermore, we're afraid to look too closely at this game or any of the others we play because we don't want to look at ourselves.

I once heard a comment about the parable of the lost sheep which fits here: "The lost sheep didn't run away. He simply nibbled his way out of the pasture and then woke up lost." We, too, can become lost with small, "unconscious" decisions. Sooner or later the consequences of our behavior will catch up to us.

We Become Dominant in Our Relationships

This game takes one of two forms, depending on the sex of the person involved. First, for a man, the game could be called "might makes right." He strives to prove his masculinity to the world by seeing how many times he can "score" or how many "notches" he can have on his belt. The media encourages this game by telling us men that our self-worth is tied to our sexual prowess. For a woman, the game could be called "seduce to prove." Her goal is to prove her femininity to the world by proving herself attractive to a man. A woman may try to earn this response from a man—and she may do so at the sacrifice of her body.

From either the masculine or feminine perspective, this behavior is a game because people become objects. They become potential conquests necessary for our own sense of achievement and significance. Sexual activity equals conquest and we are in control. Or are we?

We Believe That Thoughts of Marriage Justify Sexual Involvement

Even when it's only the second date! When we start to play this game, we're already using people for our own gain. We then proceed to use the sacrament of marriage as a ticket for our own "moral protection."[4] What becomes important for us is not the relationships, but our own needs—both our sexual needs and the need to remove any guilt we may feel as a result of such behavior.

We Get Caught in the "Good Ol' Days" Syndrome

This is the game of continuing a sexual relationship with our ex-spouse. Statistics tell us that 30 percent of divorced couples continue their sexual relationships, another 30 percent talk about the possibility, and still another 30 percent think about it. Why is this a game—and a popular one at that? Because, again, we are still drawing our identities from relationships that no longer exist. Soon this behavior will lead us to resent the situation or to fantasize that the sexual relationships can be good enough to restore our marriages; we avoid the need we have to look at why the relationships collapsed in the first place.

We Use Our Bodies as Payment for Something We Want

Ellen walked into my office one day and was direct about her purpose. "I need to know about sex," she said.

"What about sex?" I asked.

"I'm in a relationship," she explained, "and we have a regular sex life. But I don't like sex."

"Why, then, have you chosen to have sexual relations?" I wondered aloud.

"Because," she said sadly, "I need to be held, and that's the only way I can get him to hold me."

Ellen was caught in the game based on the premise that sex is a commodity given in return for something else. We all have the need to be held, the need to be touched, the need to be cared for, the need to be important. Our bodies often become the payment in exchange for a warm touch or affectionate hug.

A HEALTHY PERSPECTIVE ON SEXUALITY

Why have we spent time looking at these games? For the very same reason we have looked at other ideas and behaviors throughout this book. First, we cannot move forward until we acknowledge where we are; we must also admit that we are prone to be game-players and that we need help in dealing with our sexuality. As long as we play games, we maintain an unhealthy focus on our sexuality. Our focus is no longer on nurturing relationships but on devising self-serving ways to meet our needs. We have also looked closely at these games because they can subtly eat away at our relationship with God and with people—and they can hurt us in the process.

What, then, are we to do about the sexual part of us? Keith Miller phrases the question for us:

> How can we face our strong sexual needs, stay close to God, and make choices and decisions about our lives which will be more likely to bring us closer to God rather than take us further away from Him?[5]

Other questions also come to mind. Can we choose to be pro-life in our decisions? Do we, of necessity, need to be driven to playing games with our sexuality? Are we victims? If we have chosen to try to avoid sexual relationships outside marriage, where do we turn for a healthy, positive expression of our sexuality? Understanding the games we're prone to play, what can we do to keep from falling into those patterns? In light of our desire to avoid games and to experience God's wholeness without denying our sexuality, how are we to live?

Let me suggest six guidelines for a healthy (pro-life) perspective on sexuality.

Decide Who Will Control Your Mind

The decisions we make about ourselves and our bodies ultimately come back to this one foundational question: "Who or what owns me?" As we've seen before, whoever owns us gives us our identities. Whoever owns us provides a basis for our decisions. Whoever owns us determines our value systems.

Who or what owns you?

- Your need for affection?
- Your guilt?
- Your past?
- Your dependency or need for remarriage?
- Your ex-spouse? (As one person expressed it, "I often do things just to keep up with her and sometimes to get even with her!")

As always, not to decide about something is to decide. If we fail to put someone or something at the control panel, our decisions will be governed by our emotions, by our "needs," or by various games. If we don't make a decision about who is in control, we leave the control of our life up for grabs.

As we consider who will be in control, we must remember that God wants what is best for us. His desire to sit at the control panel of our minds is intended for our good health, not our discomfort. Nevertheless, we often avoid this decision because we see God as an avenging judge. C. S. Lewis reminded us that "God knows our situation; He will not judge us as if we had no difficulties to overcome. What matters is the sincerity and perseverance of our will to overcome them."[6]

The truth is that God cares for us and He has our best interests in mind. Our understanding of the outworking of our sexuality begins with this belief. Andrew Greeley's insights are helpful.

> If Reality is benign or gracious, then it is ultimately safe to take and be taken because no matter what happens, a gracious Reality will protect one. If, on the other hand, Reality is malign, capricious, arbitrary, then love is a risky business and surrender bound to end in disaster . . . . I would argue that he who is a Christian, that is to say, one who is fully committed with his total personality to the revelation of God as contained in his words through Jesus Christ, does not hesitate; he is on the side of Father Teilhard's interpretation. While the thought of conquest and surrender may strike terror in his heart, the terror is not strong enough to stop him. I am not saying that only the Christian is capable of friendship; but I will say that a convinced, committed Christian has a far better motivation, a far deeper rationale for friendship than anyone else. The Christian knows that the Really Real is gracious.[7]

Talk Directly to God about Your Struggles and Choices

If God is to sit at the control panel of our minds, it will be important to develop an ongoing relationship with Him. This means that we can talk to Him and tell Him our needs, our struggles, our failures, and our hurts.

Why is this so hard for us to do? Because most of us feel as if we need to promise God we will never fail again. To avoid making that promise, we simply avoid God. We may avoid Him, for example, because of our pride. We may be afraid to admit that we are weak and that we need His help in making decisions.

We may also avoid God if we picture Him as a judge who accepts us only on the basis of performance. We may have believed the myth that says we earn God's approval. It's time to discard that myth and replace it with the proper picture of God. Far from being completely removed and waiting to punish us for our failures, God sent Jesus to understand the temptations we face. Furthermore, He greatly desires to walk with us through our decisions, our struggles, and our mistakes.

Determine that Only Pro-Life Behaviors
Are Best for You

We have defined pro-life behaviors and choices as those which produce completeness, health, peace of mind, and an environment of nurturing.

If we truly believe that God wants what is best for us and that He wants to see us fully alive, then we can choose to believe that pro-life behaviors are possible. We will realize that we're not stuck in or confined to the games we're prone to play. We can make ethical choices based upon a desire to be healthy and fully alive.

Legalism says that everything is either black or white. But when we understand that God wants what is best for us, we can change our ethical question from "Is it right or wrong?" to "How can I, with fears and weaknesses, begin to live a pro-life lifestyle?" Primarily, we can stop arguing with God and begin to realize that He stands with us and wants to help us make healthy decisions.

In our weakness, however, we fall short of this ideal harmony with God's voice and direction. Our weakness and sin, therefore, result in estrangement from God, from others, and even from ourselves. But, as Keith Miller observes, "Jesus evidently didn't want people to neurotically concentrate on 'not sinning,' but rather to focus on loving God and people."[8] We don't have to wallow in memories of sin or be paralyzed by the fear of sinning again. We can instead turn to God for His guiding presence. We can decide that pro-life is best and then act according to our choice to be pro-life people.

Choose Pro-Life Environments

Having decided that pro-life behaviors are best for us, we need to move one step further by living as if that were true. In our minds, we may want to make pro-life choices, but we cloud the issue and make life very difficult for ourselves when we choose to spend our time in environments which are not conducive to pro-life decisions.

The result is all too common: "I wanted to say no, but it wasn't possible." In other words, "I put myself in a place where it was going to be extremely difficult to uphold my choice for a pro-life behavior." Assuming we can say no whenever we want to is naive, and so we set ourselves up for defeat. We need to realize that our decisions are decisions about circumstances. If our intent is to abstain from sexual intercourse, for example, the time to decide is not in the middle of a passionate embrace!

Of course, let's not kid ourselves by saying that these choices are easy or enjoyable. It's quite difficult to choose pro-life circumstances. We need to remind ourselves that the payoff (e.g., "I'm sure glad I made that decision!") comes after the decision. And that payoff is always worth the effort!

Know that Failure Is Not the Final Word

For most of us, a discussion on sexual ethics is difficult because we fear and maybe even anticipate failure. We also believe that with each failure we become less worthy as people and that God seeks ways to punish us for our "weakness." These ideas are simply invalid! We need to see that such views of God prevent us from being free from our past, from accepting forgiveness, and from the possibility of moving on.

The Bible never makes the absence of failure a criterion for the Christian or for the fullness of life Christ wants to give us. But neither is failure ignored. In the Bible, failure is redeemed. People who have failed are made whole again: they are forgiven, made new, and offered another chance.

It is also clear from the Bible that what is important is not what goes into a person, but what comes out of a person. What does that mean to us? It means that being a Christian (being pro-life, being Christlike, being fully alive) is a matter of the heart. As soon as we have focused on our failures and our capacity to fail, then we find our identities wrapped up in those failures and in the past. God wants us to leave those failures in the past, and He asks us to be His children by a choice of our hearts.

God also wants us to go to Him in an act of repentance and receive His forgiveness. As we make that choice to go to God, we know that our relationship with Him is bigger than the power of our failures. To continually hold up our failures before God would be an act of pride. It would be saying, "God, I don't believe You can forgive me, so I will let this failure be my identity." Not believing that God will accept us unconditionally, we let our failures become our identities.

Failure is not the final word. Grace is available and forgiveness is possible. Because of forgiveness, we can say, "Last night I failed. Because God has forgiven me, though, today offers new possibilities for wholeness." We can choose to live lives that are whole precisely because we are free to fail. In that freedom, we sense the possibility that our sinful, unhealthy, anti-life desires can be changed and conformed to His ideal for us. And in that freedom we sense God's presence as He allows us to pick up the pieces and grow to be more like Him.

> But the gospel of grace says that God does not stand against me, that he is not and never will be my enemy, and that he has so arranged things by the mystery of Christ's death and resurrection that at any time, before, during, or after any of my sins, past or future, I can come to him just for the coming and find myself forgiven.[9]

Commit Your Sexual Needs to God

The basic reality is that you and I were created sexual beings. Daily we deal with questions relating to the expression of that sexuality. What are we to do?

If it's true that we can talk to God about our sexual needs and if it's true that failure is not the final word, then we believe we can choose to commit our sexual needs to the Lord. With such a commitment we are saying, "Jesus, You are my Lord, my manager, my owner, and the source of my identity. You understand me and my sexual needs. You've been there before! Knowing that it is Your desire to protect me from the thoughts, attitudes, and behaviors which will be harmful to me and my growth, I commit my needs to You."

Having made that commitment, we now need to believe that Jesus is on our side. We need to believe that Jesus is ever willing to forgive us. We need to believe that Jesus walks with us and actively works to promote life. We need to believe the words of 1 Corinthians 10:13:

> No temptation has overtaken you except such as is common to man; but God is faithful, who will not allow you to be tempted beyond what you are able, but with the temptation will also make the way of escape, that you may be able to bear it.

God does not desire that we repress our sexual needs. He does not desire that we ignore them. He does not desire that we become slaves to them. Instead, He wants to redeem us and our sexuality. He wants to make us whole!

---Chapter Twelve---

Remarriage—Leaving the Past Behind

*T*he question was unexpected. "Is your remarriage a free choice?" My immediate response was, "Of course." But the more I thought about it, the more I wondered. For in reality, most people do not choose remarriage "freely." The same can be said for most new relationships. We're in bondage to

- a need for new partners to fulfill us.
- a need to undo past failures.
- a need to prove something to our ex-spouses.
- a need to be needed.

I have discovered that we ask divorced people the wrong questions. We either ask—or are asked—"Is your divorce biblical?" or "Do you have scriptural freedom to remarry?" Why is it that no one asks, "Are you in an environment where you can be nurtured, supported, and healed?" I believe Jesus is a lot less concerned about theological freedom than He is about emotional and spiritual freedom.

To focus on when or whether we may remarry is to avoid the real issue: we are in pain and need personal healing.

Statistics are not very encouraging. Eighty-five percent of divorced men and 76 percent of divorced women remarry, most of them within twelve to fourteen months. Of those who remarry within the year, more than 70 percent end their marriages in divorce. Remarriage is a reality. And my question is simple: where can divorced people become equipped to build healthy relationships?

Harold Ivan Smith is right when he observes:

> One of the primary missions [of the church] is to help those who have failed to get back on their feet, better equipped to build strong, redemptive second marriages. It's clear from the statistics that the vast majority of those divorced will remarry. That leaves us in the church with the option to either ignore them, hoping the remarriage issue will go away, or to provide a healthy, supportive fellowship that can encourage and allow second marriages to be a magnificent expression of God's healing from brokenness. When we don't provide this support, we in fact become party to the spiraling rate of second and third divorces.
>
> Unfortunately, the first option has been exercised too often. Due to our silence, avoidance, or timidity, we have encouraged many dating couples to avoid re-marital counseling and thus to make judgments that lead them to premature, unhealthy second marriages. The vicious cycle continues.[1]

Too many of us see remarriage as a convenient escape from the ongoing difficult task of paying our emotional bills. As long as we have someone in our lives, we must be okay and don't need to do any more work on ourselves. Nothing could be farther from the truth. The process of healing does not end when a new relationship begins. Granted, new relationships can begin before we have our "emotional act completely together." But healthy relationships can only begin with two individuals who are in the process of building healthy identities.

We want to rush to the shopping mall of life and go immediately to the department of relationships, hoping that we can find a significant other who will rescue our egos. In our haste, we have forgotten something. Before we leave the mall, we must pay the price that is required. Are we willing to pay the price? How high will it be?

Let's look together at some of those price tags.

We Need to Pay Our Emotional Bills

Beginning again is a matter of emotional freedom. We don't enter relationships in a vacuum. We take with us many "masters": people, places, circumstances, and attitudes that own us and tell us who we are. Those masters determine the way we relate to new people in our lives.

What are some of these "masters"? Unresolved bitterness or resentment is one. In fact, bitterness is one of the most effective poisons for killing a new relationship. If we have axes to grind, scales to balance, or wrongs to right, then we need others to support our need for revenge. We build our new relationships on the bond that we are fighting a common enemy—our ex-es. What happens when the enemy is gone? Our relationships collapse.

Our inability to forgive is carried into new relationships. Grudges work like cancer. They occupy our thoughts, our energy, and our time. The new relationships pay the price.

> Grudges can unite people. . . . Often, a divorced man and his new wife hold a grudge against the former wife: by focusing on her as the enemy outside, they can avoid the anxiety of dealing with things they don't like in each other or their marriage.[2]

We clearly must pay our emotional bills. How do we do that? We begin with taking inventory of the attitudes and emotions that own us before we enter our new relationships. I've listed a few below. Do any apply to you?

- need to forgive
- need for revenge
- need to be rescued
- fear of being alone
- need to rescue (common to co-dependents of alcoholics)

Such attitudes or emotions are not all bad in and of themselves. In fact, they're normal. But they must be identified before any change can take place.

After we identify our needs we must find nurturing environments where those needs can be addressed. This is the painful part. I need to put myself in a place where I can work on Terry. You must put yourself in a place where you can work on you. I assumed all along that the success of any new relationship depended upon my "finding the right person this time." Such an assumption made sure I never stopped long enough to do what Gail Sheehy calls the "tough repair work from the inside."[3] Finally I had to face what William Bridges calls the "neutral zone,"[4] a time of moratorium from the "busyness" of my life so I could tend to my important inner business. Although this was necessary for healing and growth, it was difficult to do because I no longer felt "productive," and I was afraid of what I'd discover if I was alone too long.

What are some practical ways to walk through a neutral zone? To find a nurturing environment for doing our inner work?

As we discussed earlier, support groups are vital. Find a group of people who are wanting to walk through the experiences you're walking through. Use this book as a reference or guide.

Keep a journal. Record your emotions and reactions. Don't evaluate them, just record them. Pay attention to the signals your emotions send you.

Don't be in a hurry. The neutral zone takes time. How much time, you ask? I don't know. But I do know that if you don't pay attention to the past (and pay your emotional bills), you're destined to repeat it.

We Need to Assume We Do Not Know All the Answers

It's called humility, approaching life with the realization that there are no guarantees. That's difficult to do. We want answers. We want our questions resolved. We want everything nice and neat. Assuming we've learned all the lessons we needed in our previous relationships is too easy. Such is rarely the case. Once a man visited me who wanted me to marry him to his fourth wife. But he refused to go through counseling with me. I asked why. He replied, "Because I've been married enough to know what to expect." I didn't marry him. And I heard later that the marriage lasted less than a year.

Because I am remarried, I am often asked about the subject. People say, "Terry, you've already messed up one marriage, how do you know this one will last?" I used to get defensive and give five or six reasons why I was sure this one would last. Then I realized that none of my reasons was valid. Now I answer their question with the only true answer, "I don't know if this marriage will last." That may raise some eyebrows, but it's a true statement. You see, I *knew* my first marriage would "last forever." I never used the word *divorce* in my house, and consequently, my wife and I never talked about problems or conflicts because doing so implied we had a shaky marriage. Before long, we didn't talk at all. And the inevitable happened.

You see, if we don't know that our new relationships will last forever, then we're going to want to work on them. If we don't know that we'll have our wives (or husbands or friends) tomorrow, we'd better love them or say "I'm sorry" or "I care" today. Today is the only day we have.

When we approach new relationships looking for guarantees, two things happen. First, we avoid all problems. Why? Because problems mess up our guarantee. Conflict becomes our enemy, and we keep waiting for the conflict to be over so we can get back to our relationships.

Second, we easily become resentful of our new partners because we expect them to be almost perfect. After all, they're responsible for guaranteeing the success of our relationships.

Why must we pay the price of recognizing that life has no guarantees? Because we need to know that we do not have to run from conflict and difficulty. Problems do not need to be our enemy.

We Need to Learn the Proper Motivation for Beginning New Relationships

What is the proper motivation for establishing a new relationship? Someone once asked me whether it was possible to marry for all the "right reasons." The answer is probably not. At least I haven't met anyone who was able to. But that doesn't mean we should avoid the sometimes messy work of being honest about the wrong motivations we have for beginning new relationships. I've listed a few. Can you relate to any of them?

- I assume that the other person exists for me.
- I assume that I know what's best for that other person.
- I assume that if it's the "right person," problems can be avoided.
- I assume that this relationship will alleviate my loneliness.
- I assume that the other person can meet all my needs.

Such assumptions and motivations are normal. But each one of them can provide the seeds for disappointment or resentment. The proper motivation does not come from pretending that the wrong ones don't exist. On the contrary, it comes from replacing them with a better motivation. That better motivation is the desire to be a servant.

That's right—a servant. A healthy marriage or friendship begins with servanthood. We need to recognize that we don't own our new partners. Unless we do, we get off track and bad motivations develop. Servanthood says, "I am a steward, and I desire to create an environment wherein Christ can work in us." My partner does not exist to make me okay. And I do not exist to "shape him/her up."

How do we learn servanthood? By practice. Lots of practice. This is also why premarital counseling is so important. It gives us a context to look at the improper motivations we will be tempted to use and provides some tools to examine the conflicts that arise because of such wrong assumptions.

I wish it were easier. But I didn't make the rules of life. Healthy relationships aren't easy. They take work. But once we realize that, we can begin to accumulate the tools necessary to help us with the work that is necessary.

We would be making a tragic mistake if we ended this chapter with the assumption that remarriage is the goal for someone who has "recovered" from a divorce. Remarriage is not the goal. Wholeness is the goal.

Some people actually feel guilty because they don't want to consider remarriage. That's too bad. They have no need to feel guilt for such an understandable desire. The principles in this chapter are not an invitation to remarriage, but a recognition that new relationships begin—sometimes when we least expect them. And it's important to begin them on the right foot.

Is it easy to pay the price for healthy relationships? No. Is it worth it? You bet.

---------- Chapter 13 ----------

Beginning Again—There Is Life After a Relationship Ends

M any years ago the English Duke of Portland owned a magnificent vase, a truly brilliant work of art. The Portland Vase, as it was called, was its owner's prized possession.

As he admired it one day, a thought came to the duke's mind. "Beauty such as this should be shared with the world. I want to loan the Portland Vase to the British Museum for everyone to enjoy."

The vase was soon prominently displayed at the museum, and the immediate public acclaim of the vase gave the duke a great sense of satisfaction.

Shortly after the opening of the display, the duke found it necessary to dismiss one of his most trusted employees. The servant was so deeply hurt by this that he sought some means of revenge, some way to bring pain to the duke.

Then he thought of the vase. Overnight, he traveled to London and paid the few pennies admission to see the vase. Planning his moves very carefully, he waited until there were no other visitors in the display room and the eyes of the guard were turned away. Carefully he crept under the protective ropes, picked up the vase, and dashed it to the ground.

The servant was quickly captured by the guards, and shocked museum officials sealed off the display room, leaving the broken pieces strewn across the floor.

When the duke was told what had happened, he immediately ordered that none of the pieces be touched. Even the tiniest chips were to be left where they had dropped. Then in Stoke-on-Trent, the pottery capital of England, the duke searched for someone who would attempt to put the vase back together again. One craftsman after another turned him down. Everywhere he went he was told that the job could not be done.

The duke was close to abandoning his search when he went to one last shop and told his story one last time. To his surprise, this craftsman agreed to try the restoration.

"But why are you willing to try?" the duke inquired. "Everyone else has turned me down. I can't understand."

"Your Lordship, my father made the Portland Vase. The pieces on the museum floor are all that is left of his finest work. I must try to rebuild my father's masterpiece."

And so, working at the museum day after weary day, the craftsman added a piece here and a sliver there. At times he despaired that the job would ever be done. Then, finally, he was finished.

The duke was overjoyed at the results. "It is a masterpiece," he exclaimed. "A second masterpiece, more beautiful now than it was before."

Once more the great vase was put on display. And once more the doors to the display room were thrown open so that the world could see the great vase.[1]

It may be difficult for us to believe that the pieces of our lives can be put back together again, but, like the duke's broken vase, your life and my life can be restored after a relationship ends.

This healing process can be a difficult one because we spend much of our time either being or feeling "out of control." We are

- bullied by our emotions,
- conned by our circumstances,
- whipped by our guilt and "if only's," and
- manipulated by our fantasies about the future.

Any discussion about tomorrow—much less about the long-range future—causes more discouragement as we imagine all the ways we will have less control than we do now. Often, as I am counseling people who are going through a divorce, I'll look at them and say simply and firmly, "There is life after divorce." Their response is usually something like, "I can't really believe that." Then I respond, "But I'm not asking you to believe it—only hear it."

In the midst of intense and varied emotions, we need to hear the affirming reality that there is life after divorce, that there is life after an important relationship ends. We may not see it, feel it, or believe it—but we do need to hear it. Why? Because that truth at least needs to touch our center of control.

As a guiding metaphor for moving on after a relationship ends, think of your life as a journey. On a physical journey you need to take a pack complete with food, water, and a medical kit. So, too, in our lives we need to pack a survival kit for recovery. In it we will put those things that will allow us to face obstacles, understand our destination, move on after accidents, and yet travel lightly. Often, people who travel for a week pack enough suitcases to last a month! I remember missing a train in Europe because I was slowed down trying to carry extra baggage full of those "necessary" souvenirs I had purchased.

The same thing can happen in life. Like the train, life can pass us by as we fumble with excess baggage full of those "necessary" souvenirs from our past. All we need, however, is a basic survival kit. What shall we put in this survival kit? I would like to suggest six items of importance; each item is a choice we make and each one affects our belief system.

KEEPING THE RIGHT ONE IN CONTROL

I can't stress enough the importance of this concept. Remember that it is who owns you that makes you important. Who does own you? The answer to that question will determine your ability to deal with the past, to relate to your ex-spouse, to understand forgiveness, and to move ahead with your future.

How do we make this important decision? We focus on the reality that He who owns us is bigger than what is going on around us. Let me give you an example from the Bible. Remember when Jesus asked Peter to get out of the boat and come to Him on the water? What happened? Peter actually began walking on the water. It wasn't long, though, before he fell. Why? Because he took his eyes off Jesus and looked at the waves and the water. We do the very same thing. As soon as we take our eyes off God and focus on the waves in our lives, we begin to sink.

When we decide who sits at the control panel of our minds, we aren't saying that the circumstances around us are not real. Quite the contrary! They are real, but they don't have power over us. We are under the care and protection of One who is greater than our circumstances, our failures, and our emotional ups and downs.

> **Affirmation Exercise:** God owns me and is sitting at the control panel of my life.

We all tend to remember our failures rather than our successes during this period of time. We therefore need to be especially sensitive to the positive steps we take toward recovery. These steps may come slowly but we need to be ready to affirm them when they do happen in our lives.

One woman was trying her best to convince me that she was failing at the divorce recovery process. "After all," she said, "I've gone two whole weeks and still haven't gotten over my depression!"

"You were depressed twenty-four hours a day, seven days a week?" I asked.

"Well," she conceded, "there was a time last Tuesday when I experienced some positive feelings about myself."

"How long did that last?" I asked.

"About an hour and a half," she said.

"That's great!" I told her. "You went from twenty-four hours of depression to only twenty-two and a half hours of depression. That's growth!"

What's the point of this story? The important lesson is that we need to see growth as taking place in small (sometimes very small!) steps. If we fail to see growth in this way, we may easily be like this woman who was unable to see any growth at all.

How, then, do we affirm our growth? We affirm it by being thankful. When was the last time you thanked God for a positive experience or a lesson learned or an affirmation of His presence in your life? An attitude of thankfulness allows us to see what God is doing inside of us, in spite of what's going on around us. Thankfulness is a conscious decision to look for growth and affirm it when we see it. It becomes a habit only when we practice it.

THE ABILITY TO SET GOALS

Often we think of growth as being merely spontaneous. "It will just happen," we say to ourselves. It's as if we expect growth to "descend" upon us one day. That is not exactly the way it works. Growth, healing, and recovery do not happen spontaneously. Just as no weight loss happens without sweat and no tumor is removed without a painful operation, no recovery or healing comes without effort.

In earlier chapters, we looked at various aspects of the divorce recovery process. Growth will take place in our lives as we implement what we have learned. One way to begin implementing these guidelines is to set goals. When we set goals, we make the statement that we are planning for growth.

When we set goals, we allow our dreams to take shape. How, though, do we set goals? We begin with a long-range goal built on the question, "If nothing were preventing me, what would I like to see happen?" Consider, for instance, this goal: "I want to be in control of my emotions." In order to measure our progress toward a long-range goal, we can use short-term goals as milestones. These short-range goals will help us define what needs to happen so that we can reach our long-range goals. Again, our example will clarify this point: to "know I'm in control of my emotions" (a long-range goal), "I need to understand my anger" (a short-range goal).

To achieve this short-range goal, we define and move toward an immediate goal. We may, for instance, set this goal for ourselves: "I will identify those things that make me angry." If we follow this method of breaking large goals into smaller goals, the setting of goals becomes a manageable process of taking one step at a time.

When I took piano lessons as a child, I wanted to be a success someday but I didn't want to practice! I'm no different today. Practice can be difficult and often it's far from enjoyable. It requires work and time and perseverance. If I don't practice a skill, though, I choose to live with certain consequences.

In divorce recovery, those consequences are discontent, self-pity, and anxiety. Basically, we become unhappy people. We avoid these consequences, though, when we choose to practice positive self-talk. Initially, we may not believe any of the affirmations we tell ourselves, but slowly and surely these ideas will take root in our lives and produce the fruit of growth and change and hope.

THE ACCEPTANCE OF OUR GOD-GIVEN FREEDOM TO FAIL

Fear of failure is one of the biggest obstacles to personal healing and growth, and this fear is both preceded and followed by self-pity. Ironically, much of our fear and self-pity may set itself up as somehow being noble: "Look at me, poor martyr that I am. I will take on the suffering of the world." What appears to be noble in fact turns out to be a means of escape: we want to escape the responsibility of change and decision making.

This desire to escape suggests that we have not yet accepted the freedom to fail. We have believed the myth that says we need to earn God's love and approval and that if we fail He surely won't approve of us! We may even begin to collect reasons that somehow justify God's disapproval. We sabotage relationships and decisions, we set ourselves up for failure, and then we say, "See! I told you God wouldn't approve!"

God's acceptance of you and me, however, is not dependent upon our success or failure. He accepts us unconditionally. Because of that, we are free to fail. What does that mean? It means that failure will not disqualify us from God's love. Failure will not take away the opportunity to start again. Failure cannot determine our ultimate identity. There is a power bigger than failure. That power is God's love for you and His love for me.

Because of this love, we can risk, make decisions, start again—grow. We can move on. We are free to fail.

THE GOD-GIVEN FREEDOM TO TAKE ONE DAY AT A TIME

We discussed earlier that most of our worries pertain to yesterday and tomorrow. We have, however, been given only one day—today! And what happens with today depends upon the choices we make now.

"But what if I make a bad choice and waste my today?" someone asked.

"You have a choice," I responded. "You can choose to learn and grow from that mistake, or you can choose to let it tell you who you are, feel sorry for yourself, and be immobilized by fear. It's your choice!"

How will you face your today? Will you start to live one day at a time, allowing each day to hold for you new opportunities for growth, for learning, for a greater understanding of God's love?

I recommend that you begin each day with this prayer: "God, You have given me today. Thank You for that gift. Allow me to see You and Your love. Allow me to risk and to learn from my failures. Allow me to grow. I am looking forward to what You have in store for me today! Amen."

A Final Word

I f you were looking for magic in this book, I'm sorry. There's no magic wand here. But there is hope. Hope that healing is not a pipe dream or an unreachable castle in the air. You really can grow through your failure, your divorce, the breakup of a significant relationship, or the death of your spouse. But beginning again—wholeness—is not a possession. It is a journey that begins today.

On numerous occasions you will be discouraged or will want to give up. At times you will fall short of your goals. There will be people who think it's their job to remind you of your failures and your feelings of guilt will be so strong you'll wonder if there's any reprieve. And there will be times when you'll no longer care about anything and you'll do your best to shut out the rest of the world. Is your journey worth it? Is there hope? The answer is a resounding yes. That yes stands on the foundation that God promises to be faithful to the task of making you whole even in a mixed-up, confused world where everyone is often unfaithful. Toward that end, he leaves you with two gifts for the journey. As this book draws to a close, I remind you of those gifts.

Failure can be redeemed.

I've always been bothered that the church often seems devoted to forcing people to wallow in their failures. "It is for true repentance," say some. "It is a reminder so that they will not repeat their sins," say others. Or, "It is an example to younger people of the consequences of sin." So we keep people in bondage to their past with reminders, innuendoes, prohibition from certain areas of ministry, and periodic references to God's judgment.

Why are we afraid of grace? Why are we afraid to let the word of Jesus set us free? Why are we afraid to hear that failure is never the final word? Is it because we will lose our system of bookkeeping that allows us to collect points of merit (or martyrdom—as a source of merit by suffering) to be used for eternal reward? Is it because we will have to be loved for no good reason—and we will have no reason to perform?

Again, Robert Capon captures the essence of this good news.

> The gospel of grace says that God does not stand against me, that he is not and never will be my enemy, and that he has so arranged things by the mystery of Christ's death and resurrection that at any time, before, during, or after any of my sins, past or future, I can come to him just for the coming and find myself forgiven.[1]

Did you say that such a promise is hard to believe? That's fair. It is hard to believe. That's why we need continual reminders. We have bad memories when it comes to such truths. How do we jog our memories? We listen to the promise, then live as if it were true. Again. And again. And again.

Affirmation Exercise: The weakness in myself can become a strength for others.

God not only says that failure is never the final word, but that your area of weakness will become your area of strength. Where you were weak and learned grace will become a place where you can reach out and touch the lives of others who need the same good news. That may sound impossible at this point. And that's okay. But the truth remains. God is not only working to heal you, but to heal others through you, to make you what Henri Nouwen called a "wounded healer."

Such healing doesn't happen through the man or woman who has all the answers. It happens through the man or woman who understands pain and grace. Nouwen explains:

> For a deep understanding of his own pain makes it possible for [the wounded healer] to convert his weakness into strength and to offer his own experience as a source of healing to those who are often lost in the darkness of their own misunderstood sufferings.[2]

A presence of joy

Joy isn't something you look for or manufacture. It's a by-product of the peace of God. It isn't an emotion or a sense of ecstasy. It is a deep sense of gratitude for life. Where does joy come from? How is it manifested?

Joy is a choice, a choice to receive the gift of God's peace. We miss joy because we usually make other choices that close our lives to the possibility of joy. We choose bitterness. Resentment. Anxiety. There's a sign on the Alaska-Canada Highway that reads, "Choose your rut carefully, you'll be in it for the next 100 miles." Have you chosen your rut? Is it busyness? withdrawal? revenge? self-pity?

Joy began to show itself in my life when I made the choice to be open—if only in a small way—to the possibility of God's peace. Karl Barth said that "joy is God's defiant nevertheless." Whatever is going on in your life may be a tragedy; nevertheless joy (or God's peace) affirms that tragedy can be overcome.

> **Affirmation Exercise:** Joy is not the absence of pain,
> but the presence of God's peace
> in the middle of pain.

Granted, joy only comes in glimpses, but with it comes hope. And because of that hope we can choose to celebrate life. Have you looked around you lately to find places where joy has invaded your world? Where joy has touched your ordinariness? The smile of a baby. The smell of brewing coffee. The warm hug of a friend. The crackle of a fire on a cold evening. The expanse of the stars. The sound of laughter with friends. The feeling of tears after a good movie. The comfort of a new book on an evening alone. Ordinary life. And the presence of an extraordinary God who gives you that life as a gift to be celebrated.

There's a humorous and pointed story about a general who asked his lieutenant for a report on the position of the enemy. The lieutenant returned in an hour. "A report on the enemy, sir. The enemy is to the north of us. The enemy is to the south of us. The enemy is to the east of us. The enemy is to the west of us. That's good news, sir." "Good news, lieutenant?" "Yes sir. They can't get away from us now, sir!"

The truth is that we walk this journey of beginning again surrounded by enemies. Enemies to the north—decisions and behaviors we wished we'd never made or done. Enemies to the south—actions done to us that were unfair or were outright wrong. Enemies to the west—our sense of insecurity and need to be loved. Enemies to the east—our fear of the future and of ever risking again. The enemies are real.

But we have a promise that is even more real: "He who is in you is greater than he [enemies] who is in the world" (1 John 4:4). That promise can so easily become a cliché and that's unfortunate. But the fact remains that we have a God who is committed to the task of making me whole and of making you whole. And He will not quit working on us until He has finished. In the meantime—on the journey—He invites you and me to celebrate.

I'm convinced that one way we do that is through humor. Humor, it has been said, is the "great exorcist." I agree. We need to laugh. At ourselves. At our predicament. With our friends. Laughter reminds us that there's more to reality than our problems and pain.

So welcome to the journey of beginning again. Laugh often. And receive God's promises that failure can be redeemed and joy can be your choice. Above all—celebrate. My friend Tim Hansel puts it this way: "There is no box big enough for life, but that God cannot flatten the sides, tear the top off and make a dance floor on which he invites us to celebrate life."

You may find the contents of this book somewhat overwhelming. That's okay. You're not being judged on how well you apply the principles given here. This book is not another reason to feel guilty. It is an invitation to live, to receive life from a God who will not quit on you.

Now, may I propose a toast? Here's to beginning again. Let's celebrate!

Notes

Chapter One

1. Gail Sheehy, *Passages* (New York: Bantam, 1977), 154.
2. Abigail Trafford, *Crazy Time: Predictable Stages of a Divorce* (New York: Harper & Row, 1982), 4.

Chapter Two

1. M. Scott Peck, *The Road Less Traveled* (New York: Touchstone, 1980), 92.
2. Sheehy, *Passages*, 238.

Chapter Three

1. Robert F. Capon, *Between Noon and Three* (New York: Harper & Row, 1982), 121.

Chapter Four

1. Capon, *Noon and Three*, 174.

Chapter Five

1. Dwight H. Small, *The Right to Remarry* (Old Tappan, N.J.: Fleming Revell, 1977), 22.
2. Smoke, *Growing Through Divorce* (Eugene, Ore.: Harvest House, 1976), 94–5.

Chapter Six

1. Smoke, *Growing,* 81–2.
2. Al Martinez, "Idaho Youth Slain by Other Prisoners—Mother, Trying to Avenge Son's Death, Sues Jailers," *Los Angeles Times,* Nov. 28, 1982, 1.
3. Barbara Lang Stern, "Your Well Being," *Vogue,* February 1983.

Chapter Seven

1. Mel Krantzler, *Creative Divorce: A New Opportunity for Personal Growth* (New York: New American Library, 1973), 51.
2. William Bridges, *Transitions: Making Sense of Life's Changes* (New York: Addison-Wesley, 1980), 90–1.

Chapter Eight

1. See Bruce Larson, *Believe and Belong* (Old Tappan, N.J.: Fleming Revell, 1982), 25–26.
2. Lee Steiner, *Where Do People Take Their Troubles?* (Boston: Houghton Mifflin, 1945), 105.
3. Clark E. Moustakas, *Loneliness* (Englewood Cliffs, N.J.: Prentice-Hall, 1961), 34–5.
4. Henri Nouwen, *The Wounded Healer* (Garden City, N.Y.: Doubleday, 1972), 92.

Chapter Nine

1. Gail Sheehy, *Pathfinders* (New York: William Morrow, 1981), 163–4.
2. Andrew M. Greeley, *Sexual Intimacy* (New York: Seabury Press. 1975), 161.
3. Sunny Pultzer, "After the Divorce: Where Have All the Friends Gone?" *Los Angeles Times.*
4. Calvin J. Fredrick, "Coping with Disaster, Many Can't," *Los Angeles Times,* Jan. 14, 1983, 22.

Chapter Ten

1. C. S. Lewis, *The Four Loves* (New York: Harcourt, 1960), 169.
2. Much of this section is adapted from Jim Smoke's *Growing Through Divorce* (see pages 33ff).
3. Sheehy, *Passages,* 182.

Chapter Eleven

1. Donald Nicholl, *Holiness* (New York: Seabury Press, 1981), 46.
2. Greeley, *Intimacy,* 41.
3. Ibid.
4. Keith Miller and Andrea Wells Miller, *The Single Experience* (Waco, Tex.: Word, 1981), 225.
5. Miller and Miller, *Single,* 229.
6. C. S. Lewis, *Mere Christianity* (New York: Macmillan, 1960), 92.

7. Greeley, *Intimacy*, 28–9.
8. Miller and Miller, *Single*, 228.
9. Capon, *Noon and Three*, 147.

Chapter Twelve

1. Harold Ivan Smith, *Salt* newsletter, vol. 1, no. 6, March 1984, 1.
2. Barbara Lang Stern, "Your Well Being," *Vogue*, February 1983.
3. Sheehy, *Pathfinders*, 314.
4. Bridges, *Transitions*, 114.

Chapter Thirteen

1. Patricia Chavez and Clif Cartland, *Picking Up the Pieces: Reshaping a Life Torn by Divorce* (Nashville: Thomas Nelson, 1979), 155.

A Final Word

1. Capon, *Noon and Three*, 147.
2. Nouwen, *Wounded Healer*, 87.

For Further Reading

Augsburger, David. *Caring Enough to Forgive, Caring Enough Not to Forgive.* Ventura, Calif.: Gospel Light, 1981.

Bridges, William. *Transitions: Making Sense of Life's Changes.* New York: Addison-Wesley, 1980.

Capon, Robert F. *Between Noon and Three.* New York: Harper & Row, 1982.

Greeley, Andrew M. *Sexual Intimacy.* New York: Seabury, 1975.

Hart, Archibald. *Feeling Free: Effective Ways to Make Your Emotions Work for You.* Old Tappan, N.J.: Fleming Revell, 1979.

Krantzler, Mel. *Creative Divorce: A New Opportunity for Personal Growth.* New York: New American Library, 1973.

Larson, Bruce. *Believe and Belong.* Old Tappan, N.J.: Fleming Revell, 1982.

Lewis, C. S. *The Four Loves.* New York: Harcourt Brace Jovanovich, 1960.

Lewis, C. S. *Mere Christianity.* New York: Macmillan, 1960.

Miller, Keith and Andrea Wells Miller. *The Single Experience.* Waco, Tex.: Word, 1981.

Moustakas, Clark E. *Loneliness.* Englewood Cliffs, N.J.: Prentice-Hall, 1961.

Nicholl, Donald. *Holiness*. New York: Seabury, 1981.
Nouwen, Henri J. M. *The Wounded Healer: Ministry in Contemporary Society*. Garden City, N.Y.: Doubleday, 1972.
Peck, M. Scott. *The Road Less Traveled*. New York: Touchstone, 1980.
Sheehy, Gail. *Passages*. New York: Bantam, 1977.
Sheehy, Gail. *Pathfinders*. New York: William Morrow, 1981.
Small, Dwight Hervey. *The Right to Remarry*. Old Tappan, N.J.: Fleming Revell, 1977.
Smoke, Jim. *Growing Through Divorce*. Eugene, Ore.: Harvest House, 1976.
Steiner, Lee. *Where Do People Take Their Troubles?* Boston: Houghton Mifflin, 1945.
Stoop, David. *Self-Talk*. Old Tappan, N.J.: Fleming Revell, 1982.
Trafford, Abigail. *Crazy Time: Predictable Stages of a Divorce*. New York: Harper & Row, 1982.

Discussion Questions and Exercises

Chapter One

1. What do you think we can learn from our emotions?
2. Is handling your emotions difficult for you?
3. Finish this sentence: Some of the emotions I am feeling are . . .
4. With which of the four stages of beginning again can you most identify?
5. Is there one area where you are struggling or hurting more than others? What is that area?
6. Finish this sentence: I have hope because . . .

Chapter Two

1. What is the first step toward growth after a marriage has ended?
2. List some of the "myths" that hinder growth. Can you add any of your own to the list?
3. Why would people want to hope that the beginning-again process might be like "magic"?
4. Why are "war stories" not particularly helpful to beginning again?
5. What, according to the author, is a sign of true strength?
6. True or false. Healing from a broken relationship will make things as though the divorce had never happened. Explain your answer.

Chapter Three
1. Who or what are some of the people, places, or attitudes that "own" you?
2. What are some of the stumbling blocks to getting to know yourself?
3. What are some of the things that cause you to resent life?
4. Is it difficult to believe that God loves you unconditionally? Why or why not?
5. Finish this sentence: My goal this next week is to work on (something that relates to helping you have a positive identity).
6. Finish this sentence: I should be glad that . . .

Chapter Four
1. Do you sometimes wonder where God is?
2. How do you feel about the fact that sometimes God doesn't seem close to you when you need Him?
3. Do you need to "feel good" about God before you can approach Him? Why or why not?
4. What are four guidelines for "moving on" with your life?
5. What was your reaction to the talk the author had with Bob?
6. Is it possible for God to be with you even when you think He is silent?

Chapter Five
1. Briefly summarize what the Bible has to say about divorce.
2. Why is the statement, "I can never be used by God again!" nothing but selfish pride?
3. Why is Peter such a good example of God's grace?
4. How does genuine repentance begin?
5. Do you think that God can offer us renewal before we acknowledge our failures and ask for forgiveness? Why or why not?
6. Why are growth and struggle necessary for healing and wholeness?

Chapter Six
1. Finish this sentence: For me, the most difficult part of the forgiveness process is . . .
2. Do you find yourself wanting to blame someone else for your problems? Who?
3. Have you given up your "right" to hurt back?
4. Which of the "fantasies" listed on pages 80–81 do you struggle with most? How do you intend to deal with them in the future?
5. Have you asked your ex-spouse for forgiveness? Why or why not?
6. True or false. You are not forgiven until you feel forgiven. Explain your answer.

Chapter Seven
1. What are the principles of self-talk?
2. Finish this sentence: I have difficulty letting go of . . .

3. Finish the following sentence: My self-talk reinforces that difficulty when I tell myself . . .
4. Finish the following sentence: I can change my self-talk by saying . . .
5. How is positive self-talk different from wishful thinking?
6. Have you set up a self-talk goal for yourself? Who will help you achieve your goal?

Chapter Eight

1. Are you feeling lonely now?
2. Make your own "loneliness is" list. (See page 100.)
3. How have you tried to "solve" the problem of loneliness?
4. Does the author feel that you can find a permanent solution to the problem of loneliness?
5. In what ways may loneliness be a gift?
6. In what ways are you going to reach out to other lonely people?

Chapter Nine

1. Has a situation similar to the one that happened to Gail Sheehy ever happened to you? How did you react?
2. What is a friend?
3. Name some of the things friends can do for us. Name some of the things friends cannot do for us.
4. What attracts friends?
5. How would you define a support group?
6. List some ways support groups can help you work through the issue of loneliness.

Chapter Ten

1. Describe your current feelings toward your ex-spouse. (Use only *one* word!)
2. How would you like to feel about your ex-spouse? (Again, use one word.)
3. Which of the Steps mentioned do you find yourself most easily tempted by?
4. Which of the six growth guidelines for coping with your ex-spouse is the easiest for you? Which is the most difficult?
5. What, for you, is the most difficult area of the process of detachment (making a clean break)?
6. Finish this sentence: My self-talk for this week is . . .

Chapter Eleven

1. What does it mean to be a "body person"? Do you agree or disagree with the author's point of view?
2. What does the author mean by "pro-life" behavior?
3. What are some of the games that divorced persons play?
4. Finish this sentence: I see God as . . . (Loving Father, angry judge, etc.)

5. Why is it important to put God at the control panel of your life?
6. Finish this sentence: One area of weakness that I have that requires change is. . .

Chapter Twelve

1. Are you acting as if you are a captive to your past? Or are you accepting and truly believing that Jesus forgives you?
2. When can a healthy relationship begin?
3. What is a neutral zone?
4. Name some things a support group can do for you.
5. True or false. If I marry the "right person" problems can be avoided. Why or why not?
6. Can all of our needs be met by a new relationship?

Chapter Thirteen

1. Who owns you?
2. How do you set your goals? What are the biggest problems you have in setting them?
3. What goals would you like to set for yourself in the following areas—money, job, personal and spiritual growth, relational development, parenting?
4. Joy is a _____.
5. Finish this sentence: If I knew that I could not fail, I would attempt . . .
6. Finish this sentence: About my future, I feel . . .